Essential Nursery Management

'Susan Hay is an outstanding leader in the field of Early Childhood Education. The nursery chain she developed is perceived by the field to be offering outstanding services and her book is written in a way which really speaks to early years practitioners in training and to practitioners in key management roles.'

Margy Whalley, Director of the Pen Green Research, Development, Training and Leadership Centre

This new, fully revised edition of *Essential Nursery Management* recognises the huge changes that have taken place in public policy and parental awareness, which have inspired practitioners to strive for quality and sustainability in their childcare provision.

Written by a highly acclaimed expert in the field, this practical and accessible book addresses all the critical aspects of effective nursery management, from leadership skills and one-to-one skills, developing and monitoring the curriculum and staff training and appraisals, to astute financial management, marketing strategies and evaluating a nursery's services.

Susan Hay takes a close look at the political and social context in which childcare services are provided today and asks:

- What do parents expect?
- What do employers want for their workforces?
- What rights do children have?
- How can childcare providers work together for the benefit of children and families?

Supported by 'real-life' case studies, examples of policies, procedures and rotas that can be adapted by the reader, and written with a non-prescriptive approach, this book will be invaluable to anyone wishing to fully engage with the demanding role of managing any early years settings, whether as part of studying at GNVQ or Foundation degree level or in day-to-day practice.

Susan Hay was previously Executive Director Europe for Bright Horizons Family Solutions, an international group of nurseries operating in the US, UK, Canada and Ireland. She is currently a freelance consultant.

The Nursery World/Routledge Essential Guides for Early Years Practitioners

Books in this series, specially commissioned and written in conjunction with *Nursery World* magazine, address key issues for early years practitioners working in today's nursery and school environments. Each title is packed full of practical activities, support, advice and guidance, all of which is in line with current government early years policy. The authors use their experience and expertise to write accessibly and informatively, emphasising through the use of case studies the practical aspects of the subject, whilst retaining strong theoretical underpinnings throughout.

These titles will encourage the practitioner and student alike to gain greater confidence and authority in their day-to-day work, offering many illustrative examples of good practice, suggestions for further reading and many invaluable resources. For a handy, clear and inspirational guide to understanding the important and practical issues, the early years practitioner or student need look no further than this series.

Titles in the series:

Circle Time for Young Children
  − Jenny Mosley

Developing Positive Behaviour in the Early Years
  − Sue Roffey

Identifying Additional Learning Needs in the Early Years: Listening to the Children
  − Christine Macintyre

Understanding Children's Development in the Early Years: Questions Practitioners Frequently Ask
  − Christine Macintyre

Observing, Assessing and Planning for Children in the Early Years
  − Sandra Smidt

Drama 3–5: A Practical Guide to Teaching Drama to Children in the Foundation Stage
  − Debbie Chalmers

Music 3–5 (forthcoming)
  − Susan Young

Encouraging Creative Play and Learning in the Early Years (forthcoming)
  − Diane Rich

Learning and Playing Outdoors (forthcoming)
  − Jan White

Thinking and Learning about Maths in the Early Years (forthcoming)
  − Linda Pound

Supporting Multilingual Learners in the Early Years: Many Languages – Many Children (forthcoming)
  − Sandra Smidt

Essential Nursery Management

A practitioner's guide

Susan Hay

Routledge
Taylor & Francis Group

LONDON AND NEW YORK

NURSERY
WORLD

First published 1997
by Baillière Tindall

This edition published 2008
by Routledge
2 Park Square, Milton Park, Abingdon, Oxon OX14 4RN

Simultaneously published in the USA and Canada
by Routledge
270 Madison Ave, New York, NY 10016

Routledge is an imprint of the Taylor & Francis Group, an informa business

Typeset in Perpetua by
Florence Production Ltd, Stoodleigh, Devon
Printed and bound in Great Britain by
TJ International Ltd, Padstow, Cornwall

British Library Cataloguing in Publication Data
A catalogue record for this book is available from the British Library

Library of Congress Cataloging in Publication Data
Hay, Susan, 1951–
    Essential nursery management: a practitioner's guide/
Susan Hay. – Rev ed.
        p. cm. – (Essential guides for early years practitioners)
    1. Nursery schools – Great Britain – Administration.
    2. Day care centers – Great Britain – Administration.
    I. Title.
    LB2822.7.H39 2007
    372.21'6068 – dc22   2007011492

ISBN10: 0–415–43071–2 (hbk)
ISBN10: 0–415–43072–0 (pbk)
ISBN10: 0–203–93907–7 (ebk)

ISBN13: 978–0–415–43071–5 (hbk)
ISBN13: 978–0–415–43072–2 (pbk)
ISBN13: 978–0–203–93907–9 (ebk)

The book is dedicated to Alex, who was my own son's keyworker, and who left my company to set up her own, in the north-east of England. Her energy and tenacity has taken early years to another level.

Contents

Illustrations

Preface

Management is about ensuring that every moment of everyone's time is invested shrewdly – that is, in the most effective way possible. It is about ensuring that something more worthwhile could not have been done in place of what was in fact done: no waste, clear focusing, pinpointing, routines to ensure smooth operations, no more people than necessary.

The nurturing and education of very young children does not easily recall such skills and attitudes.

To what extent can 'normal' management approaches help, in the endeavour to provide good early years' services? This question requires us to look at who the stakeholders are in early years' services. There are a number of them – all with differing priorities and different reasons for being involved:

- the parents, whose overriding concern is to achieve the best start in life for their child;
- the child, who must settle, enjoy for its own value his or her time at nursery, and who must benefit from the development and learning opportunities;
- the regulatory body acting within its statutory duty to ensure provision is safe and sure;
- the staff who seek a rewarding role;
- the driving force, who may own the business or lead the voluntary organisation, whose passion is responsible for the existence of the provision, and who may also manage the nursery;
- the shareholders in a larger organisation who will wish to see a return on their investment;

- developers who are concerned that the 'amenity' they have accommodated makes sense in terms of their real property interests; and
- employers who will be monitoring the impact of a nursery provision on their workforce.

This is probably not an exhaustive list, but it serves to illustrate the range of priorities that the main stakeholders will have. It follows that the services we provide must also differ, in order that they respect and include all stakeholders' interests and emphases. We cannot and should not deny such differences.

However, we can and should find ways of holding on to both sets of essential values: values of good childcare and values of good management.

This book is essentially a discussion of the 'non-negotiable' aspects of early years' services management. How can we resolve the impossible daily dilemma of quality versus costs? How can we ensure that services of quality are delivered within a planned management framework, one that allows them to be stable, permanent and to thrive?

Not one of the very different stakeholders' interests is served by lack of management: there is neither a future in charging so little for a service that, despite everyone being able to afford it, costs are not covered; nor any in charging so much that an excellent service can be ensured yet for most parents is prohibitively expensive.

A balance has to be struck – a balance you can live with. This is the aspect that is hard for those involved, and much harder – and much scarier – than for those with most other types of small business. Here, the foundations of early learning are being cast, and we now know that the future life chances of young children are determined by the quality of their early years' experience.

This book aims to link the components of good management with the components of good childcare. I have attempted to take up from where most professional training for early years' practitioners leaves off, drawing heavily on my own experience of running a group of nurseries. I am indebted to all of the recognised thinkers in both fields and have drawn, in particular, from Charles Handy, Bob Garratt and Andy Hargreaves on management, and from Margy Whalley, Loris Malaguzzi and Elinor Goldschmied on early years.

The book is for all those who want to sustain a good childcare business and motivate others to do the same.

Acknowledgements

All photographs were taken at Bright Horizons' nurseries in the UK and are used with grateful thanks to children, staff, parents and the company.

I would like to thank Bright Horizons Family Solutions for generously allowing me to use some excellent examples of practice, and the Daycare Trust and Working Families for opening my eyes to the broader issues surrounding children and families.

NOTE

Asterisks have been used to indicate where the full reference is included in the 'Bibliography and references', pp. 193–5.

Introduction

Developments in early years policy and provision over the last few years have been overwhelming in their importance for young children and their families. The issue has taken centre stage for the government and is built into the narrative of the press. The high profile that early years policy has enjoyed has secured it a place in every household's conversation, and has placed it on the agenda of human resources (HR) professionals, bankers and investors alike; there are now accountants and estate agents, insurance brokers and architects specialising in the early years sector. The most recent legislative initiative, the first-ever Childcare Act 2006, has enshrined

in law the expectation that all parents in the UK can now have of accessing high-quality early years provision.

The radical moment was the publication of the government's Green Paper, *Every Child Matters**, in 2003. This followed the tragic deaths of several children, including Victoria Climbie, deaths that enquiries had shown could have been avoided if appropriate practices were effectively in place. The Green Paper's central purpose was to make sure that our most vulnerable children are protected. Awareness of the problem of children falling through the cracks of a system that was not joined up led to an exploration of why children who are experiencing difficulties of all kinds at home and at school were receiving too little help, often too late. *Every Child Matters** was concerned with improving children's lives as a whole, both protecting them and maximising their potential. It set out a framework for services for children from birth to nineteen, some of which are universal and some of which are targeted at groups with specific and additional needs. It set out five key outcomes that mattered most:

- being healthy;
- staying safe;
- enjoying and achieving;
- making a positive contribution;
- economic well-being.

It introduced the concept of Sure Start Children's Centres in the most deprived neighbourhoods and promoted the idea of extending school hours to offer before- and after-school care. It made proposals for:

- supporting parents and carers;
- early intervention and effective protection;
- accountability and integration locally, regionally and nationally;
- workforce reform.

Ten Year Strategy for Childcare: Choice for Parents, the Best Start for Children* was published by the government in December 2004. This set out the challenges for policy makers and practitioners in improving parents' choices about balancing work and family life. It supported the widely held belief that the fastest route out of poverty for families is through work, and therefore positioned childcare as a critical plank in achieving a reduction in poverty. But it went further, and heralded the establishment of Children's Centres in every community, not only the most deprived. Together with the earlier Nursery Education Grant* initiative for three and four year olds, this marked a genuine commitment to universal pre-school care for all children. The strategy also acknowledged that education and care for the youngest children could be brought together in a more coherent way; specifically, the strategy committed the government to introducing a new single quality framework for children from birth to five. Crucially, the strategy made clear the government's intentions to devolve responsibility for commissioning children's services to local authorities, which would assume a market development role rather than one of direct provision, thereby securing an opportunity to participate for public, private and voluntary providers.

The *Childcare Act* 2006* has paved the way for the necessary structural changes to be made to achieve the government's aims, and comes into force in 2008. The key points of the Act are:

- It introduces the *Early Years Foundation Stage**, requiring all settings offering provision for children from birth to the beginning of Key Stage 1 to provide integrated care and education. This brings together and replaces the *National Standards for Under 8s Daycare and Childminding**, *Birth to 3 Matters**, and the National Curriculum Foundation Stage.
- It places a legal duty on local authorities to secure sufficient childcare places in their area, including places for children of working parents, through a mixture of provision.
- It introduces a new OFSTED (Office for Standards in Education) register for all services for children from five to eight years old, to ensure minimum standards of safety.

The Act places early years provision in the mainstream of local authority activity, and requires local authorities to ensure appropriate and sustainable services for the whole of their community. For the early childhood profession, it heralds a new perception of those who work with young children, placing them on an equal standing to those who work with older children. For providers, it gets rid of the false distinction between education and care.

Although the last few years have felt like 'initiative overload', the *Childcare Act**, mentioned above, marked the beginnings of the move away from a culture of short-term, target-driven testing for young children, and a return to the soul and spirit of young children's experience of learning.

The reality as this book goes to press is that there is still only one early years place for every three children under eight, although occupancy rates are generally low. Although the use of early years services is rising for all groups, it is rising more slowly for under-represented groups such as children of lone parents, certain black and ethnic minority groups and low-income families. For parents of disabled children, there is precious little provision at all that suits their needs. And early years services are still unaffordable for many, with parents still required to contribute approximately 75 per cent of the full cost.

We know that a quarter of average household income is now spent on early years services, where they are used. We also know that what stops a parent from using childcare provision when it is available and they can afford it is the trust they have in the provision. This is why we should welcome the *Childcare Act's* attempt to raise the quality bar and acknowledge that care and education should never have been separated for young children. Our services must be of high quality, otherwise parents will not use them; they must be as efficiently delivered as possible in order that parents can afford them and in order that they are sustainable over time. We should add another finding – that employers want more and more flexibility from their workforce and, indeed, that working parents want this, too, to balance their work and family lives. This presents providers with the challenge of offering flexible early years services, the kind that keep up with and reflect the way people want to work and run their lives now.

Early years services in the future need to reinforce the dual responsibility of ensuring that the cost of the service is linked to improving the quality of outcomes for children in which parents can have confidence and of securing the right investment from other stakeholders to render the service affordable for parents. These stakeholders could be: the government, which has big aspirations to realise; local authorities, which need to maximise the benefit to their communities; developers, who want to attract buyers and tenants into their schemes with the right and most important facilities; employers, who possibly have the most to gain beyond parents and children themselves, through the well-proven business case for retention and well-being of staff.

Understanding the changing context in which early years services are provided is part of providing sustainable leadership in a nursery setting. This book does not prescribe how to run your nursery, but draws heavily on my own experience over the last sixteen years of trying to find feasible ways of going beyond the expectations that others have of us:

- Chapter 1 looks at the nature of nursery management. How do we approach things differently now we have accepted the role of leading the team, and on what does developing such an approach rely? What makes a manager a leader?
- Chapter 2 looks at the important management issues and how these can be dealt with effectively.
- Chapter 3 looks at what is involved in leading a team, and how it affects the leader.
- Chapter 4 looks at staff as an investment – how we find, nurture and develop them personally and professionally.
- Chapter 5 looks at the leader as the nursery ambassador – how to present and promote the service offered and identify what is important to families.
- Chapter 6 looks at the support and guidance offered by the construction of a plan, treating the nursery as a small business and measuring progress.
- Chapter 7 looks at moving the service forward, adapting to change and remaining agile to remain sustainable.

In this book we use 'nursery' as an all-embracing term for any group setting that will require registration under the Children Act, where children under five are receiving early years services. 'Nursery' includes day nurseries, Children's Centres, pre-school playgroups, after-school provisions, Extended Schools services.

If there is one message I wanted to put across, it would be that profit with principles can be achieved. Profit is our oxygen, principles are our blood: we need both for our health.

Chapter 1

Who is a manager and what is management?

- Management and leadership
- Fit to manage in the eyes of others
- Manager's rite of passage
- Maturing as a manager
- Are nursery managers born or are they made?
- Trust in leadership

Leaders are called to stand in that lonely place between the no longer and the not yet and intentionally make decisions that will bind, forge, move and create history.

We are not called to be popular, we are not called to be safe, we are not called to follow. We are the ones called to take risks, we are the ones called to change attitudes; to risk displeasure. We are the ones called to gamble our lives for a better world.

Mary Lou Anderson, Address to the
House of Delegates, April 1970

The success of a nursery will depend on a range of factors but it is clear that there will be a heavy reliance on the quality of its leadership. A frequently-quoted belief is that 80 per cent of deficiencies in nursery services relate to weaknesses in leadership. This may be a generalisation; however, there is no doubt that strong and effective leaders are critical in securing good outcomes for children and families.

MANAGEMENT AND LEADERSHIP

People who are selected or are identified as nursery managers are used to managing. The care and education of young children inevitably requires organisational skills, setting expectations of behaviour, maintaining standards, evaluating outcomes – all the issues normally covered in professional qualifications and training for nursery nurses and teachers. However, this innate experience does not seem to translate easily when it comes to applying it to the nursery as a whole, and it does not necessarily translate into leadership.

Management of a nursery, in my view, encompasses both management as it is usually thought of, and leadership – which is generally believed to be something broader than management. Leaders are people who can influence the behaviour of others for the purpose of achieving a goal. Leaders possess a special set of rather baffling qualities that enable them to persuade others to do what the leader wants because they want to do it. Leaders can balance concern for the task, for quality and for efficiency, with equal concern for the people they work with and the relationships between them.

Managers are understood to be concerned with routine and focusing on the present. Their actions are usually dominated by issues of continuity and stability, and they are responsible for efficient control of finance, for sensitive management of staff and families, and for maintaining the reputation of the nursery. There are now a number of management qualifications offered that complement nursery nursing, and employers will increasingly expect manager candidates to have achieved such a qualification. Acquiring

7

a qualification to lead is more elusive. The differences between leadership and management have been noted by Hodgkinson (1991)*:

- leadership is an art whereas management is a science;
- leadership is focused on policy whereas management is concerned with execution;
- leadership is concerned with values whereas management looks at facts;
- leadership is generalist, management is specialist;
- leadership uses broad strategies rather than management's specific tactics;
- leadership is concerned with philosophy rather than action;
- leaders are reflective, managers are active;
- leaders are concerned with human resources whereas managers are concerned with material resources;
- leaders focus on deliberation, managers on detail.

In most nursery settings the manager is indeed required also to be the leader. The financial constraints of having two people at this level usually require both roles to be filled by the same individual and it is probably only within the larger nursery groups that you begin to see the distinction emerge. The syndrome of having to deal with both roles is often described by management consultants as management of the 'important versus the immediate', where important refers to those big value-based issues with which a leader is concerned, vying for time with the manager's need to respond to day-to-day problems that constantly arise.

While it is true that in order to be an effective leader you need to be an efficient manager, management skills do not equate with leadership skills – they are much wider. Also, although having highly developed management skills will probably allow you to create time for leadership functions as well, having poorly developed management skills will inevitably prohibit attention being paid to leadership functions. This book uses 'management' to describe the combination of leadership and management required in nursery settings. However, with the advent of nursery groups, including those operated within schools and Children's Centres, the nursery is often part of a group, with a support network of regional management that limits the extent of leadership expected of the nursery manager. The relationship between the manager and those who are identified as leaders then needs careful attention, and must be clearly communicated.

Illustrating how leadership and management come together for those in early years' services, Gillian Rodd (1994)* lists the essential characteristics for the job:

- *Curiosity* (interest in learning);
- *Candour* (open to public scrutiny and willingness to speak the truth);
- *Courtesy* (respect and dignity for others);
- *Courage* (willingness to take risks, dare, make mistakes);
- *Compassion* (creating trust and empathy).

But there is an alternative view of leadership, which is that unlike the manager, a leader can exist at any and all levels in a nursery team. 'Leaderful teams' is a concept developed at Pen Green Research, Development & Training Base and Leadership Centre, and discussed at more length in Chapter 3: Leading a team and managing a service.

It would also be argued by many that a nursery manager's role should embrace all those responsibilities traditionally associated with leaders, and that the edges between the two are blurred, i.e. a good manager must also be a good leader. Indeed, under the *Every Child Matters** agenda, the DFES (Department for Education and Skills) identifies seven aspects of management/leadership as necessary core competencies in championing children, a shared set of skills, knowledge and behaviours for those leading and managing integrated children's services (2005):

- achieving outcomes;
- safeguarding and promoting the welfare of the child;
- providing direction;
- leading and managing change;
- working with people;
- managing information;
- communicating and engaging effectively with children, young people and families.

This development can also be evidenced in recent initiatives such as the *National Standards for Leadership of Children's Centres*, published in spring 2007 by the National College for School Leadership (NCSL)*. The standards are grouped into six key areas, which are both interdependent and of equal importance, and come together around the essential purpose to improve outcomes for children and families (see Figure 1.1).

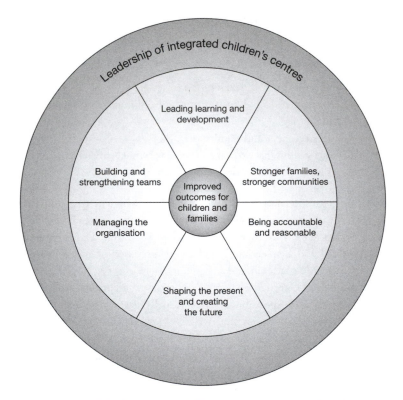

FIGURE 1.1 NCSL*: National Standards for Leadership of Children's Centres

Source: National College for Schools Leadership

NCH, the National Children's Charity, formerly, National Children's Home, considers that leadership and management must be combined in the role of nursery manager in order to maintain a culture that remains true to its values of having a sustainable future, delivers high performance and demonstrates the value placed on each person's contribution:

- providing leadership and direction;
- working in partnership;
- delivering excellent results;
- motivating and managing people;
- making a personal impact;
- being accountable;
- learning and sharing.

This new approach to the role of the head of a nursery has been largely driven by the evolution of the Children's Centre programme within the *Every Child Matters** agenda that by definition requires a broader and higher level of professional expertise and aptitude than has been expected before, both by regulators and parents. Even though some nurseries may consider that they are not asking the same of their managers, there should be no difference in the sense of responsibility that the post holder feels and takes on: children, families and staff deserve no less from the individual in charge on a day-to-day basis. All nurseries need to be aspirational, if only to compete in the recruitment market for the best staff.

FIT TO MANAGE IN THE EYES OF OTHERS

The National Children's Bureau's (NCB) *Guidelines for Good Practice in Group Daycare* (1991)* describes the management responsibility as:

- ensuring that the nursery is operating smoothly;
- responding to the needs of parents, children and staff;
- being open to suggestions for development.

These three points encapsulate the essential needs for:

- policies and procedures to be understood and followed;
- staff to be empowered to make decisions that are flexible to changing needs;
- recognition that new knowledge and new ideas need to be continuously assessed and incorporated into practice.

Each of these three concepts requires the manager to learn continuously: from mistakes, from other people, and from other ways of going about running a nursery.

When we combine the need for learning, and the need to develop directing ability, we create the idea of the *learning leader*. This is a more appropriate title for the person responsible for ensuring that the NCB Guidelines are met; that the service is managed in a way appropriate to a changing profile of children, a changing profile of parents, a changing staff team, new thought on how children develop, and new legislation.

The first stage is to learn from what is actually going on in your nursery. If we reflect on the circumstances that lead to such tragedies as the deaths of Victoria Climbie, and Ellie Lawrenson, they become more disturbing because the knowledge necessary to avoid this tragic loss of human life

11

lay within the hands of those responsible. If there is no system for sharing information, no real means of learning from previous experience, no process for listening to feedback from stakeholders and for communicating all this to those responsible for taking preventive action, then avoidable errors will occur.

In a nursery setting, when information does not flow freely and openly in the interests of children and parents, this can be characterised as 'oh I thought she was doing that' or 'if only you'd told me that earlier' – all contributing to destroying cooperation, encouraging buck passing and undermining instructions.

The first step for a new manager, then, is to create or review the *learning system* by which the nursery can become both more effective and more efficient. This combines the written policies and procedures, and routines for review and evaluation of practice. Both these issues are dealt with in Chapter 2.

OFSTED has a specific view, for the purposes of registering and inspecting a nursery under the Children Act, of what makes a manager and the directors of an organisation 'fit', and this should be regarded as the baseline for competence in the role.

MANAGER'S RITE OF PASSAGE

The second step is for the manager to go through an important rite of passage:

> You are now so valuable to us, that you must leave the day-to-day operation of the organisation, and have time and space to think about how effective we are in relation to the changing entitlements and needs of children and parents, what the future of those changes might mean, how we can position ourselves strategically and how we can create a system of rapid learning so that we may keep up with those changes.

In addition to their qualifications, nursery managers today are expected to have received at least induction and a significant handover period with their predecessor, if not specific training, before taking up their role as manager.

This is now an acknowledged, budgeted item. Training, however, no matter how thorough, is most likely to focus on the specifics of the job, rather than helping a new manager to assume the confidence and sensitivity required of a leader. They are still very likely to have been promoted as a result of being the best at their (previous) job. In the absence of any transition or training, it is not thought to be legitimate to develop a new role. This tends to manifest itself in firefighting the *immediate,* rather than thinking about the *important.* 'This Action Fixated rather than Action Learning approach is the curse of management', says Bob Garratt (1990)*.

Having committed yourself to the notion of action-learning, and having considered what is necessary to change your own mind from one of operative to manager, it is time to deal with the development of others. If you are to provide a consistently good service then all staff must be empowered to make decisions that provide parents and children with solutions to their needs.

It is necessary for the manager to coach, counsel and train others to do the same as you. These are the systems, provision and techniques of supervision, appraisal, staff meetings and in-service training (see Chapter 3).

How then does the whole nursery move forward? On top of the expectations we have of ourselves, based on the service we purport to offer, what of the ever-increasing expectations of others? Today's excellence is merely tomorrow's standard, and never is this more true than in the nursery world. If you *know* that children thrive under certain conditions, in certain environments, with certain principles in place, how can anyone accept second best? In this industry, there are no 'special purchases' or '2 for 1 offers'.

Embracing change and the turbulence it can cause requires maturity in a manager. Faced with the moving target of *quality childcare,* change is part and parcel of everyday nursery life. The tools that the nursery manager requires here are ones of quality assurance, sound practice, consultation.

As a team member, you are a technical specialist – a nursery nurse or teacher. As a manager you are a generalist – knowing enough about every aspect of the nursery to give direction and support. Rather than responding to the instructions and advice of others, as a manager you need to anticipate what instructions and advice others will need.

MATURING AS A MANAGER

My family was delighted, my friends were delighted if a little envious, and my staff thought that it was great that one of us had made it. The only problem was that after a few months I felt totally inadequate, became depressed and dreamt only of getting out, or back to the stability of my old job.

13

The organisation of most nurseries is that of a 'flat pyramid' – a team of nursery staff work with a manager and it is usual for the manager to have come from the team, as this move represents a promotional opportunity in an organisation where few exist. As a member of the team the individual has probably worked to a well-defined job description, with clearly identified responsibilities and tasks. Suddenly, from this position as a single-function team member, you are asked to become a 'learning leader' (Garratt, 1990)*. We talk a lot about the function of nurseries as facilitating the 'maturation' of young children, but what of the process of developing maturity in a job?

This process can be viewed as having six stages (Figure 1.2). *Induction* is a stage that is handled well in nurseries and involves introducing a newcomer to all aspects of 'the way we do things around here'. *Inclusion* is the second stage needed to mature in a job. This is a more subtle concept and rarely managed well – it is the opposite of 'being left to sink or swim' and is about being accepted in your role by colleagues. It is about personality and behaviour and conventions rather than technical ability and experience. People are rarely selected on such criteria, yet it is on these abilities that you will be included in – or excluded from – a working team. In order that acceptance or rejection is not left to the group, the new individual needs counselling and coaching and insight into what makes the group tick.

The third stage, *competence,* can be reached only if one has been fully included. Some would argue that, in being selected, the new recruit is *competent*. I would argue that competence is situational, and specific, and being competent in one setting does not necessarily mean that you will be competent in another, even though the role might be the same (i.e. nursery manager). Competence relies not only on abilities but on cooperation with others – inclusion in the group.

Once someone has been successfully inducted and included and has demonstrated their competence in the team, then they are ready to develop – bringing out what is within the individual to benefit the whole. This is often felt to be so alien to people's expectations of their job that it has to be made 'legitimate' before it can happen. Thus in the move from 'having a job' in the team to 'having a role' in the organisation, you are the kind of person that is valued by the organisation, and it is now time to contribute to how it will grow and how its culture will evolve. Through a process of self-development, an individual can add to their activities and expand their attitudes. This allows them to reset their personal targets and identify new challenges. Not only are they competent but they are

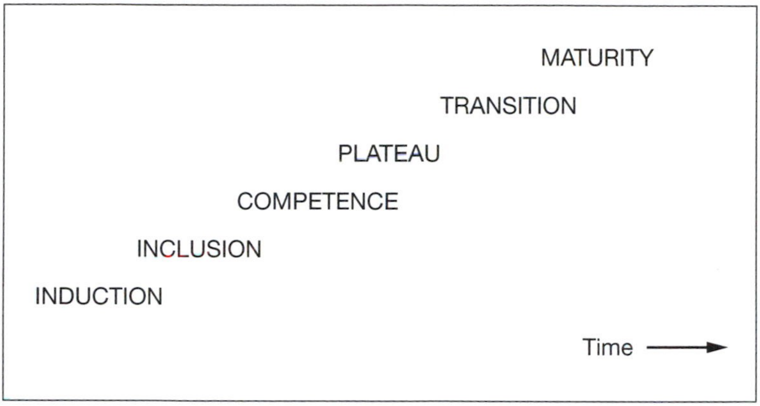

```
                                    MATURITY

                              TRANSITION

                        PLATEAU

                  COMPETENCE

            INCLUSION

      INDUCTION


                                          Time  ⟶
```

FIGURE 1.2 The process of development

also fulfilled, and able to bring their own special qualities to the job for which they are employed.

An individual reaches a *plateau* in terms of the development process when the individual, their boss and their staff are happy with the way things are going, and start resisting change. This can quickly lead to a stale working environment, or to the individual moving on! If *transition* is seen as a career change, then we are looking at promotion, redundancy, job rotation, etc.

The development process should apply to every working member of a team, but we are much better at looking after it for those who are not heading-up the team. Unless we focus on the needs and aspirations of the team leader, he or she will be limited in the leadership and managerial role: the person will keep their head down, search forever about what to do and how to do it, and begin to feel fairly wretched. It is difficult to say to your (junior) colleagues, 'Look, I am not becoming competent as your manager, I need some training.' In practice, overcoming this may mean that nursery managers must ensure that they provide this for themselves and form a network of external 'mentors'. Against the backcloth of the patchy and singular nursery industry, this feeling of isolation is often particularly acute.

The most common response, particularly if the resources of time and money for training are scarce, is to retreat into a position of comfort. To be precise, managers return to their old job, but this time unprofessionally. Relief is instant, as you slip back into old routines, language, and behaviour. But others are furious. What of the additional responsibility they had taken on when you were promoted? This knock-on effect continues down through the team, and can lead to people admitting that they are paid at a higher level than the job they actually do. The following are five specific ways for ensuring that such development blocks do not get in the way:

- Enable the manager to become involved in the review and formulation of policy, in order that it is not something simply received at the nursery level, from a management group on high, but rather that the nursery, through the manager, shares ownership of the policy change.
- Allow the manager time and space to review their strategic role, to take in and consider the impact of external changes on the nursery.
- Value and use the individual strengths of the manager, and supplement them with help in those areas in which they do not feel strong.
- Delegate problem-solving to staff team members.
- Accept that learning is continuous and free-flowing to wherever it is required.
- Use an appraisal process to develop leadership.

Such an appraisal could incorporate the following prompts for discussion:

Manager/leader appraisal grid

Leadership

- conveys a clear vision;
- initiates and drives through change;
- is visible, approachable and earns respect;
- inspires and show loyalty;
- builds a high-performing team;
- takes final responsibility for actions of the team;
- demonstrates high standards of integrity, honesty and fairness.

Management of people

- establishes and communicates clear expectations;
- gives recognition and helps staff develop full potential;

- addresses poor performance;
- builds trust, morale and collaborative working;
- delegates effectively, making best use of skills within the team;
- deals with matters face to face as much as possible;
- seeks feedback;
- manages relationships with management.

Personal effectiveness

- shows resilience, stamina and reliability under pressure;
- takes decisions in a timely way;
- is aware of personal strengths and weaknesses and their impact on others;
- offers objective advice to management;
- pursues agreed action with energy and commitment;
- adapts quickly and flexibly to change;
- invests and manages own time to meet competing priorities.

Strategic thinking and planning

- anticipates future demands, opportunities and constraints;
- demonstrates sensitivity to all stakeholders' needs;
- understands long term implications of decisions;
- translates objectives into practical and achievable plans;

Communication

- handles hostility through negotiation;
- concise and persuasive orally and in writing;
- listens to others and respects difference;
- demonstrates IT competence;
- chooses methods of communication most likely to achieve effective results.

Expertise

- earns credibility through depth of knowledge and breadth of experience;
- knows how to find and when to use other sources of expertise;

- shares and explores best practice from other settings;
- understands how policy changes impact operations and all stakeholders.

Delivery of results

- sets performance into context of stakeholders needs;
- delivers results on time, on budget and to agreed quality standards;
- ensures others organise their time to achieve objectives;
- knows when to intervene and when to step back;
- encourages feedback on performance and has a process for learning.

Management of finance and contracts

- negotiates for the right resources to do the job;
- commits and realigns resources to meet key priorities;
- leads initiatives for better use of resources;
- ensures management systems are used to monitor and control resources;
- manages contracts with suppliers effectively.

Intellect, creativity and judgement

- generates original and practicable ideas;
- justifies actions with reference to core principles;
- analyses ambiguous data effectively;
- encourages creative thinking in others;
- delegates decisions appropriately.

ARE NURSERY MANAGERS BORN OR ARE THEY MADE?

There are three schools of thought on the making of managers: Do they possess certain innate traits that lend themselves to management? Do they behave with a certain style and have an approach that sets them apart from non-managers and enables them to exert influence over others? Or is it the situation in which they find themselves – the job that needs doing – that determines their need to manage?

Although personal characteristics can help, it is now generally recognised that management skills can be learned. It is also recognised that management potential can appear at any time in a career, leading to the notion that individuals can be capable of managing different situations at different stages in their lives. The demands of the situation and the characteristics of other people in the group will then determine the management skills required at that time and the most effective management style to adopt.

TRUST IN LEADERSHIP

The role of trust in leadership is becoming more highly valued. This quote from Niall Fitzgerald, then Chairman of Unilever, sums it up: 'You can have all the facts and figures, all the supporting evidence, all the endorsement you want, but if – at the end of the day – you don't command trust, you won't get anywhere' (Hutton and Davies, n.d.)*.

Trust matters, as the cases of Enron and Farepak have demonstrated so vividly, and at times of uncertainty people want to trust more, to hold on to certainties that they feel may be slipping away. The qualities parents seek from the childcare they need, and opting for childcare at all, are, for many, one such area of uncertainty. Parents need those from whom they buy services to be as trustworthy as their friends and family. Trust is the essential glue that makes the work of leaders tenable, and enables them to compete on the basis of added value and commitment to an increasingly wide group of stakeholders, rather than on cost of services alone. Trust is a new 'must have', and is integral to the offer we make to children and families. How purposeful are we about gaining and keeping trust, or do we just assume it will continue to be there unless we break it? By living the core values of the nursery every day the leader can continuously convince stakeholders that he or she deserves their trust. This requires core values to be identified and communicated in such a way that the nursery is seen to be part of the community in which it operates. Each element of that community, from owners to staff to supply chain to parents, is as important as the next. Basing performance narrowly on satisfying one of these groups alone is not a strategy for maintaining trust.

Nurseries are, rightly, a highly regulated area of work, and we are surrounded by different groups auditing what we do. Auditors seek failure against a set of standards, which is one reason why trust has become such an important issue for childcare. Being seen to fail is bound to

19

reduce trust in the nursery service. However, this trust deficit does not necessarily indicate that nurseries are performing less well, but rather that they are (all) pursuing a standard of service that is constantly getting higher: today's excellence is only tomorrow's standard! Equally, parents' expectations are rising, as are children's entitlements, as we learn more and more about them.

Intrinsic reasons for trusting someone or an organisation are things such as personality, their values, their rhetoric; extrinsic reasons might be the other relationships they are involved in, whether they honour their promises, and what others have said about them. A breakdown of elements of trust has been developed by Paul Oliver at the London Business School:

Component of trust	Driving factor
expectation	personal values
quality of interaction	accuracy
communications	perceived appropriateness of message, medium, timing
transparency	understanding of the service; action; motivation

Management guru Charles Handy has identified seven rules of trust:

- Trust is not blind: it needs fairly small groupings in which people can know each other well.
- Trust needs boundaries: define a goal, then leave a worker to get on with it.
- Trust demands learning and openness to change.
- Trust is tough: when it turns out to be misplaced, people have to go.
- Trust needs bonding: the goals of small units must gel with those of the larger group.
- Trust needs touch: workers must sometimes meet in person.
- Trust requires leaders.

Chapter 2

Focusing on the task

- Balancing needs and expectations
- Decision-making
- Planning the use of resources
- Policies and procedures
- External pressure for written policies
- A manual of policies and procedures
- Appendix

BALANCING NEEDS AND EXPECTATIONS

A nursery manager is concerned with the needs of three main, separate, but interrelated groups of people. These are the children, their parents and the staff who are employed. However, increasingly the nursery manager is accountable not to her/himself (as owner) but rather to a management board that has responsibility for the ultimate feasibility and quality of the service provided. This may be a formal board of directors, or where Children's Centres are attached to schools this will be the school governors. For a voluntary sector setting, those with management responsibility will be the trustees of the charity that funds the nursery; and in the case of workplace nurseries, the 'steering group' will be determined by the employer that sponsors the provision. Unless the nursery manager is the owner of the setting, he/she will have delegated responsibility from the management board and will need to be clear about the level of authority he/she is assumed to have. This is important not just for day-to-day operational efficiency, but also so that parents and others contracted to the nursery (e.g. as suppliers) understand what to expect from the manager, and when they should refer to the management board. It is even more critical to clarify the manager's responsibility and level of delegated decision-making if nurseries are established through the collaboration of two or more organisations. For example, where a Children's Centre is part of a cluster servicing a community, it may be housed in one school but offering places to parents using several schools for older children: which set of governors is the higher authority, and what part does the local education authority play? Nurseries now no longer have a single point of reference: they are held to account by a number of stakeholders. An example is provided in Figure 2.1. The central issue is to establish a reporting structure that allows the nursery manager to focus on the task.

The purpose for which the nursery is established is to provide a service for children. To do this well, both parents and staff must also be cared for and nurtured, but the service is and should remain the central focus of attention. Surprisingly, this idea can get lost, and a nursery can very soon become primarily concerned with meeting parents' requirements and aspirations. Or a nursery can start to revolve around the staff and their comfort, career development and social life. Although all this is important, nothing is so critical as the confidence gained from knowing that everything you do as manager can be justified in terms of the service offered to children.

A new stakeholder group

FIGURE 2.1 Stakeholders for a workplace nursery

Source: Susan Hay Consultants

The very best situation would be one where both the quality of work (i.e. service (task) performance) and the quality of life (i.e. staff morale and parent satisfaction) are optimised. However, real life usually requires us to make choices, and I would argue that, where a choice has to be made, the service to children should not be allowed to suffer. A critical aspect of the manager's role is to raise awareness of the need, sometimes, to make such a choice, that the children's needs cannot be met in the best way if staff and parents achieve their preferences as well. So the manager must balance, as far as possible, these sometimes conflicting demands (see Case Study 1).

Striking the right balance will involve the manager in ensuring that:

- each stakeholder is asked what he/she wants and needs regularly;
- time is managed to achieve all objectives;
- strengths, abilities and contributions of staff are fully utilised;
- decisions are properly informed;
- decisions are properly communicated.

Case Study 1: BALANCING THE NEEDS OF CHILDREN, PARENTS AND STAFF

A rash had broken out in the baby unit. Over the course of two days five babies had developed a rash which, to the manager, looked like measles. However the children were not unwell. Parents were contacted and advised to take their children to their doctors. This produced a variety of diagnoses, none of measles. They ranged from 'miscellaneous viral infection' to 'non-specific allergy' and 'eczema'. None of the GPs was able to confirm that the rash was not contagious.

The parents were keen to return the children to nursery and to return to work themselves, confident with the various doctors' views that the children were not in the first stages of something more serious. However, the staff were concerned that as the outbreak had involved such a significant number of babies then further spread of infection was possible. They made efforts to isolate the children from the older group, just in case. One child in particular began to itch and scratch quite vigorously, although was not upset or considered to be unwell.

Clearly the nursery staff could not deny the advice of the GPs, but the routine in the nursery was being significantly affected by the staff's concern – based on little clear information. Understandably, parents felt there was no real need to exclude the children from nursery. One child had begun to show signs of illness. The local health authority was contacted in order to obtain a view on what action the nursery could take to identify the cause of the rash and therefore the appropriate response. It was not the nursery's role to dispute the diagnosis of a doctor, or to make a judgement on the basis of any one particular doctor's opinion.

The issues I have found to require the most attention, in order to satisfy parents' expectations as well as children's entitlements, from a management perspective are:

- engaging parents;
- settling new children at their own pace and similarly when children transition from one group to another within nursery;
- maximising individual attention for children within larger and/or more standardised settings;

- resisting the temptation to run the day by an institutional routine of meals, etc;
- working as a team so that knowledge of a child and family is shared, and the family is not vulnerable if a member of staff is absent;
- retaining the value of early childhood itself, while preparing children for school;
- preserving the personality of the nursery in the face of standardisation through regulation;
- having clear policies and procedures around children's health.

Increasingly, parents have a clear view of what they are looking for in childcare that not only meets the needs of their child but also matches their employment pattern. The recognition in the Labour Government's *Ten Year Strategy for Childcare** that flexible childcare is a key component of an appropriate service for parents provided a welcome new perspective to helping parents juggle work and family lives. The reality for parents is that one work schedule, or one childcare arrangement, will work only for a certain length of time and then it requires changing. The trigger for change can come from the needs of the child or from the parent, and often the change cannot be anticipated or it is temporary. In choosing childcare, parents increasingly need to know that as a need arises their childcare hours can change with their working hours in order that both work and family can continue to thrive. It is less of a balancing act and more one of careful management and open communication with parents. However, offering flexible childcare arrangements inevitably leads to fewer places being occupied full-time, and will lead to higher costs of provision to cover voids.

The roles and responsibilities involved in addressing these issues are dealt with later in Chapter 5.

DECISION-MAKING

Decision-making is part of everyday life in a nursery, and involves making choices. The quality of decisions made will affect the quality of the service provided, and it is the manager's responsibility to ensure that the best information available is at hand on which to base a decision. If decision-making is to be delegated in any part, then the manager must ensure that the individual to whom it is delegated is fully supported (see Chapter 4).

Available information will be consistent with the manager's experience: to what extent has a similar situation arisen before and how effective was the decision taken at that time? Equally important is the professional underpinning knowledge that the manager has to bring to the decision. Although many decisions taken in the course of the nursery day do not lend themselves easily to making a rational choice – for example, behaviour management, ethical judgements, staffing problems – and are perhaps guided more by time constraints, pressure from parents or a lack of decision-making structure within the team, it is crucial to have a manager with a high level of qualifications and experience. Indeed, recent workforce transformation initiatives from the Children's Workforce Development Council (CWDC) have paved the way for managers to be educated to at least degree level – in order that they have the analytical skills, the ability to think and plan logically, to resist the temptation to let emotional issues cloud the matter. This is becoming a recognised expectation, as was noted in Chapter 1.

I would suggest that the skills required of the manager here should relate to the structure of the organisation as a whole. If the manager is unsupported, then he/she will need such ability at her fingertips; if, however, the manager has support and direction from seniors with whom difficult decisions can be shared, then he/she is not relying totally on their own knowledge and breadth of experience, but on that of the organisation as a whole.

Routine decisions, which occur frequently, may well have a procedural solution that is well rehearsed in the nursery. They will not challenge the manager, and will require little discretion or professional judgement. This type of decision can be made by staff with reference to written guidance, providing that they understand when to consult the manager. Such a decision is based on previous success, and is sometimes referred to as a 'programmed decision'. All staff should be familiar with the response, and it should be committed to writing in a procedures manual.

A wider problem-solving approach is required for the irregular or new situation that has never been met before, or only infrequently. This may call for a spontaneous reaction, or a considered, customised decision. Such decisions are likely to be made personally by the manager. It is the differences between, rather than the standardised similarities in settings that will give rise to more decisions being taken in this way. This both acknowledges the importance of committing the programmed decisions to a manual, which everyone can follow, and of having a manager capable of rising to the challenge of acquiring decision-making skills in order to cope with a larger number of instances in which such skills will be required.

Carlisle (1979)* argued that there are three types of decision (see Case Study 2):

- *intuitive,* i.e. those led by feelings and emotions, regardless of information that might suggest a different response;
- *judgemental,* i.e. those for which the outcome can be predicted because they are based on expert knowledge;
- *problem-solving,* i.e. where time allows study and reflection before a course of action is decided upon.

Intuitive and judgemental decisions are basically taken independently by the leader unless specifically delegated. He/she is then going to be held accountable for the outcome. The problem-solving approach allows the decision to be shared, and is therefore a less risky strategy, if it can be achieved within the timescale demanded. A manager needs to select the appropriate type of decision-making to ensure that the situation is met with the highest possible quality of decision given the time available. I would add here that indecisiveness or prevarication is rarely an appropriate response where children and parents are involved; however, these are not the same as agreeing to review a policy over time.

In terms of personal risk, decision-making strategies can be ordered as follows (with the most 'risky', i.e. for which the person taking the decision is solely accountable, first):

- individual decision-making by the manager;
- individual decision-making by the acknowledged expert;
- decision-making by averaging the opinions of individuals;
- decision-making by the manager following group discussion;
- decision by a minority;
- decision by a majority;
- decision by consensus.

A good decision is one that is both right and good, and not simply expedient and practical. This is why Codes of Ethics and Codes of Practice are drawn up for members of professions. As we move towards higher expectations of managers in the UK, the next step will be to develop such codes, which encourage managers to find creative solutions to situations as they arise, but grounded in principles that others can expect them to hold firm.

Case Study 2: INTUITIVE, JUDGEMENTAL AND PROBLEM-SOLVING DECISIONS

A vacancy arose for a Senior Nursery Officer and three candidates applied, all from other nurseries within the same network. Two of the candidates had previously worked with the manager at the nursery with the vacancy, who was responsible for interview and selection. The third candidate had worked briefly in the nursery before, providing holiday cover, but at a time when the manager was herself away from the nursery.

The manager's spontaneous reaction to the three candidates was to state a preference for one of the two candidates she had worked with, and to suggest that the one she knew to be outgoing and vivacious would be the most appropriate choice. This was an intuitive decision on the manager's part. Her choice may well have been the right one: she knew her team and who would and would not fit in; she also knew what personal characteristics would contribute something important to the nursery.

However, company procedure stated that all internal candidates must first and foremost be considered in light of recent staff appraisal documentation, and their skills and experience matched to the job specification for the vacancy. This route would result in a judgemental decision — one that can be evidenced and backed up with information.

The judgemental process eliminated one candidate but did not provide a clear choice in favour of either of the remaining candidates. They both met the specification, but in different ways, and personal knowledge of the situations they were intending to vacate added a further dimension. The manager decided to find a solution in conjunction with the two managers of the nurseries they would be leaving, to discuss the pros and cons from each nursery's point of view. This was a problem-solving approach to finding the right candidate.

PLANNING THE USE OF RESOURCES

Staffing and everything that goes with it is the most essential and critical aspect of good nursery management. It has already been noted that the quality of service provided relies largely on the quality of the staff, as the manager cannot be everywhere. Staff must be capable of tuning into children's and parents' needs quickly and accurately, and understand when to involve the manager.

The staff/child ratio

The ratio of staff to children is only one aspect of adequate staffing: the 'iron triangle' of achieving quality through staff also embraces their qualifications and the size of the group of children they are caring for (Munton *et al.*, 2002)*. If one point of the triangle changes, then the other two will also require adjustment:

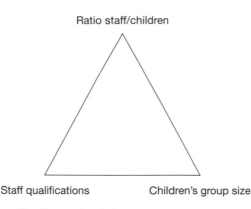

Ratio staff/children

Staff qualifications   Children's group size

 **FIGURE 2.2** The 'iron triangle'

Source: Munton *et al.,* 2002

There are many differing views on what staff ratios, according to the age of the child and size of overall group, should be, and little agreement on whether a fixed ratio fulfils the needs of children at all. In many European countries, achieving a regular and expected staff ratio takes second place to the qualifications that staff have and their ability to tune into the needs of each child; ratios do not drive the way the service is delivered. In the US, the opposite is virtually true, where minimum ratios, in every room of the nursery, is seen as critical to protect the nursery from criticism. In the UK minimum staff ratios per child have been set down and the number of children per group is limited; however, the rules are less strict in terms of separate rooms for groups. The visual result of these different approaches can usually be seen in how open plan a nursery is able to be, how free-flowing the whole space is, and the extent to which the space can be used flexibly.

US	UK	Europe
Strict ratios and group size	Strict ratios and flexible group size	Flexible ratios and group size
Classrooms	Some open plan	Open plan

What you say you do must be done. Strangely, this is often not the case. Parents will have been told that you maintain certain staff/child ratios according to the age of the children. Clearly achieving this is not in the application of an exact science, as children change age groups continuously and so the nursery has an amoebic profile, which rarely allows for ratios to be in place, in precise terms. Similarly, children move between different activities and groups in the nursery and frequently groups will exceed the stated ratio because of the popularity of the activity. The staff/child ratio is intended only as a general guide to staffing levels. It allows for child contact and non-contact time and it is highly unlikely that at any given moment the stated staff/child ratios can be precisely observed.

Again, if staff/child ratios are 'always maintained' are they really in place throughout the day? Are all absences of staff truly covered? For example, will all or some of the following give rise to covering staff: lunch breaks, coffee breaks, holidays, staff sickness, training on site and off site, shopping for the nursery, attendance at internal and external meetings, absence of the manager on other business? All these areas leave a gap in the staff/child ratio. either directly or because a member of the team is deputising for the manager.

In addition, if staff are expected to: exchange information with the next shift, undertake child observations, write up child profiles/records, supervise students, be supervised themselves, plan activities, mount artwork, meet with parents, etc., are these routine non-contact tasks absorbed into the (ratio) day? Or are staff given time out and, if so, is it covered by an additional member of staff? In recent years a much greater emphasis has been placed on planning for non-child contact time. The planning process involves observation of children, planning activities, evaluating those activities and sharing good practice, and it is now expected that staff should be able to attend to this part of their work within the nursery day.

Shift planning

For years my own company worked an 8-hour staff shift, even though our nurseries were open for 10 hours, excluding setting up and closing down time in the mornings and evenings. Because of the need to fit in all those essential absences, as well as the non-contact, on-site tasks, it was impossible to achieve an even spread of staff throughout the day and maintain a viable staff cost. We constantly battled with too few staff in the mornings and evenings, given the workload at those times, and too many staff at times of the day when we needed them least. The only solution was to over-staff, pushing up costs and inevitably increasing fees to parents.

We experimented with a staff shift of 10 hours, but maintaining a working week of 40 hours; i.e. staff work four days each week instead of five. This allowed us to plan staffing accurately against anticipated child attendance. For example, if Friday is less busy in the nursery then staff 'rest days' can be planned to coincide. The 10–hour shift also provided us with a means of achieving high levels of staff from opening to closing time, and in particular helped with the early and late periods in the day.

There are many issues to take into account when deciding on the right length of shift for your nursery, and you must assess the relative importance of each aspect:

- opening hours;
- patterns of arrival and collection of children;
- parent requirements at both ends of the day;
- variation in daily pattern of occupancy;
- staff contracts of employment;
- commuting patterns of staff;
- incidence of evening meetings;
- extent of non-contact duties;
- use of agency/temporary staff;
- physical separation of nursery rooms.

Staff costs

It is generally considered that, to achieve a high quality of service, salary costs (including agency fees or temporary staff wages) should not be less than 50 per cent of the nursery's turnover – i.e. fees received from or on behalf of parents. Without doubt, staff costs are the element of total costs that it is crucial to control: measure the effect on the economics of the nursery of a 5 per cent overspend on salary costs, against a 5 per cent variance on any other item. It is therefore entirely appropriate for staffing requirements to be driven by total fees (or equivalent) expected. Careful control of forward bookings in the nursery, and actual child attendance, are together the most prudent route for planning staff resources (see Figure 2.3). Clearly there are external factors that affect the 50 per cent minimum rule of thumb. Building in more non-contact and training time, particularly when the existing staff are expected to reach higher levels of qualification, as well as current recruitment conditions, can influence the proportion of costs expended on staff: the context of staffing constantly changes, along with the development of nursery services:

- What choice of candidates do you have?
- What qualifications do you require?
- What expectations do parents/regulators have?
- What choices do candidates have?

Clearly being offered an appropriate salary is a basic requirement of those who work. However, there is now much research that shows that the work–life balance opportunities offered by employers are the most crucial factor in choosing a job, and they are frequently quoted as the main reason for joining a particular organisation or declining an offer in favour of another. Those who choose nursery work are most aware of the needs of children and families, including their own. Strangely, as a profession the nursery world lags behind most other business sectors in addressing this increasing issue in creative ways. It is neither easy nor impossible to offer flexible work to those who are totally client-focused, as consulting and counselling service organisations have found. Finding successful ways forward does not necessarily rely on investing additional cost, but it does rely on great teamwork and the collegiate support that goes along with it, and on recruiting a balanced team to provide flexible opportunities as the need arises that do not affect the quality of overall service. The

	Mon a.m.	Mon p.m.	Tue a.m.	Tue p.m.	Wed a.m.	Wed p.m.	Thu a.m.	Thu p.m.	Fri a.m.	Fri p.m.
Total under-2s × 5 booked hrs	17	17	18	18	19	19	17	17	16	16
U2 total hrs U2 ratio 1:3	85.0	85.0	90.0	90.0	95.0	95.0	85.0	85.0	80.0	80.0
Staff hours	28.3	28.3	30.0	30.0	31.7	31.7	28.3	28.3	26.7	26.7
Total 2–3s × 5 booked hrs	11	11	14	14	16	16	16	16	15	15
2–3 total hrs 2–3 ratio 1:4	55.0	55.0	70.0	70.0	80.0	80.0	80.0	80.0	75.0	75.0
Staff hours	13.8	13.8	17.5	17.5	20.0	20.0	20.0	20.0	18.8	18.8
Total 3–5s × 5 booked hrs	5	5	5	5	5	5	4	4	3	3
3–5 total hrs 3–5 ratio 1:8	25.0	25.0	25.0	25.0	25.0	25.0	20.0	20.0	15.0	15.0
Staff hours	3.1	3.1	3.1	3.1	3.1	3.1	2.5	2.5	1.9	1.9
Total staff hours	45.2	45.2	50.6	50.6	54.8	54.8	50.8	50.8	47.4	47.4
Staff required	9.0	9.0	10.1	10.1	11.0	11.0	10.2	10.2	9.5	9.5

	Mon	Tue	Wed	Thu	Fri
Carol	1	1	RD	1	1
Mary	RD	1	1	AL	1
Alex	RD	1	1	1	1
Fiona	RD	1	1	1	1
Lorraine	1	1	1	1	RD
Karen	1	RD	1	1	1
Julie	1	1	RD	1	1
Claire	1	1	1	1	RD
Susan	1	RD	1	1	1
Tracy	1	1	1	RD	1
Joe	1	RD	1	1	1
Lynda	1	1	1	RD	1
Permanent staff	9	9	10	9	10
Agency	0	1	1	1	0
Jennifer (Manager)	1	1	1	1	1
Staff on site	10	11	12	11	11

FIGURE 2.3 An example of staff planning for one week
(AL = annual leave, RD = rest day)

recent recipient of the small business category of Working Families'
Employer of the Year Award related a story to the judges of how the
introduction of a leave banking scheme, and having an extra day's holiday
for your own or a family member's birthday, reduced turnover by 64 per
cent! Both these programmes can be planned for, and both were suggested
by staff as factors that would make the biggest difference for them.

POLICIES AND PROCEDURES

Why do we need to specify our policies and why do we need written
procedures? Surely these things deny professional judgement and preclude
imaginative response.

Providing consistency for children and parents, and empowering staff
to be flexible, is not a contradiction in terms. The first allows the second
to be approached with confidence and with the full support of the team.

The smooth running of the nursery relies on routines being respected
and achieved. There are many safeguards to put in place, particularly
stemming from health and safety regulations, equal opportunities practice,
child protection measures, local authority registration requirements and,
last but not least, the contract for services made with parents. It is an
absolute entitlement of children and parents that they can rely on all
these requirements being in place, every minute of every day. My purpose
here is not to rehearse such standard and basic elements of a nursery
service, but to look beyond entitlements of children, to better practice.

Written procedures reduce the incidence of misunderstanding as to
the standard of the measure put in place. They allow parents and staff to
predict how matters will be dealt with. They provide a basis for review
and improvement of procedures. And they do not leave the nursery
vulnerable when the person who 'knows about that' is absent (see Case
Study 3).

Written procedures reflect state-of-the-art childcare, and as such are
your defence if questioned on the standard of services you offer. It is
important that you can rely on the fact that *all* your staff will deal with
a particular issue in the same way, thus providing consistency of service.
You can be even more certain that this will happen if staff understand
why procedures have developed. What is the objective of having a
procedure for that particular nursery function or routine? This may be
particularly important for you as you look for ways of making your nursery
distinctive from the crowd that become memorable characteristics,
adding value to your service. This does not mean making a radical change

Case Study 3: A WRITTEN POLICY WOULD HELP

It was the end of February and everyone who hadn't had a cold all winter now had one. The sun had not shone for months and many children were left with lingering coughs and catarrh. They needed extra help settling for naps and kept each other awake. This was getting to be a strain for everyone, and parents were frustrated at collecting irritable children at the end of the day and going through the whole process again at bedtime. Calpol helped at home, and so it was suggested by a parent that a spoonful would also aid the midday nap. This particular child had been very susceptible to the colds going round and had had more than the average time away from nursery because of this.

The nursery had a clear written policy about the administration of prescribed drugs in nursery. It also had a clear written policy that, in the incidence of an abnormal temperature, Calpol would be given having sought the parent's specific permission, in the intervening period between telephoning the parent and the child being collected. There was no written policy about the administration of non-prescribed drugs in any other circumstances.

The parent wanted the nursery to administer Calpol to aid sleep while the child's cough continued. The nursery refused. The parent sought advice from the local authority, who considered that where a parent's permission had been specifically requested and received, then the nursery could do this. The member of staff had no written policy to support her view that it was inappropriate for the nursery to administer over-the-counter medicines except where the child was unwell. Had she had this, a heated discussion in the nursery could have been avoided as it would not have been an issue for negotiation.

to the service you offer; however, it can suggest an improvement to the way you offer it. Interestingly, making the mistake of constantly changing the menu in Little Chef restaurants to improve the loyalty of customers has proven to be the downfall of the group. With hindsight, post-bankruptcy in early 2007, the managers saw that the answer lay in the way they executed their (traditional) service: customer service and presentation. An example from nursery might be introducing a 'shoes off' policy for the whole of the nursery, and not just the baby room. The hygiene reasons for this are subject to debate; however, the attention to detail that it displays to visitors is immense.

Having written policies and procedures is now a given; however, having it in a form that can be quickly and regularly updated, and maintaining its centrality to the service in the eyes of staff, is another matter. Routines get forgotten or gradually changed and diluted over time; perhaps worse, they become so embedded in the culture of the nursery that they become too precious to change. A manual should be an unfinished, part work, capable of absorbing new expectations and new, tested practices. Advances in IT have obviously made this continuous review and development a much easier process. Most of all, the manual should become a source of pride, as much as of support.

EXTERNAL PRESSURE FOR WRITTEN POLICIES

OFSTED inspectors will now expect as a minimum that a manual covers all the areas they look at, for example:

- staffing policy, including number of staff, their qualifications and training;
- educational programme and activity;
- record-keeping, progress recording, reporting to parents;
- premises and equipment available;
- health and safety policies;
- equal opportunity policies;
- special educational needs policy and how it is implemented;
- admission policy;
- opening hours, dates and daily programme;
- discipline policy;
- fees;
- complaints procedure;
- copy of the last OFSTED report.

Receipt of Nursery Education Grant* for 3 and 4 year olds and the acceptance of tax-efficient *Childcare Vouchers**, will both depend on successful achievement of this part of the inspection process, as parents must be given the right information to enable them to choose the best childcare option for them. Moreover, nurseries must now show that they are working towards *Every Child Matters** agenda, which strives to enable all children to:

- be healthy;
- stay safe;
- enjoy and achieve;
- make a positive contribution;
- achieve economic well-being.

A MANUAL OF POLICIES AND PROCEDURES

Written procedures are best produced as reference manuals that can be readily updated. The more well-thumbed the manual, the more consistent your service is likely to be. The more familiar staff are with the manual, the more likely it is that they will contribute to its review and updating. Like any manual, it will evolve over time and be a living, learning information resource. It may begin with the fulfilment of the nursery's registration criteria, which will cover the essential areas noted earlier, of health and safety, equal opportunities, special educational needs, and child protection.

The manual should then expand to incorporate areas of good practice that are not regulated under the Children Act, and further, to include aspects of quality provision consistent with your nursery's commitment to children and parents (Figure 2.4). It is important that each procedure carries any relevant cross-references to other procedures, and that the manual is kept up to date with current information, such as names, addresses, etc.

Each policy or procedure should begin with a statement of what the objective is – i.e. for what purpose a policy or a procedure is being laid down, and for whose benefit it has been written, and why there should be a standardised way of handling the issue.

Philosophy

There should be an overall statement of the nursery's intention and approach to childcare. It can include references to the underlying principles of early learning to which the nursery relates (e.g. Montessori, Piaget, Reggio Emilia, a blend . . .) and it can explain how parents might detect that these principles are at work in the nursery. This is also where increasingly, a Code of Behaviour, or the organisation's values can be found – those principles and approach to working with children and families, and with each other as professionals, that the nursery will not be compromised on. An excellent example is provided by Bright Horizons Family Solutions, and included in full in Chapter 3.

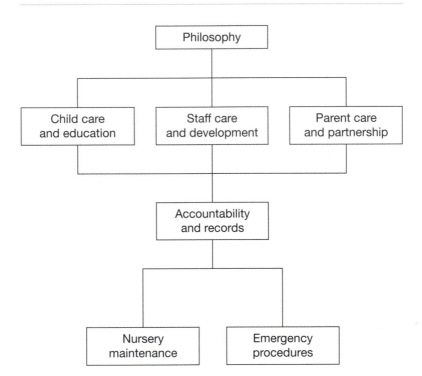

FIGURE 2.4 A framework for a manual that incorporates all standard procedures carried out in a nursery

This section should also consider the nursery's response to new thinking in child development practice and contemporary issues that concern parents, for example, the maximum hours per day and per week that you are prepared to have children in nursery for. Does your philosophy have a reference point in research, such as the UK's *Effective Provision of Pre-School Education* (EPPE)*, which did not find a direct effect on behaviour of hours of care, or the US National Institute of Child Health and Development (NICHD)*, which did find a link between more than 40 hours of care per week and minor increases in levels of 'aggression and disobedience'?

Childcare and education

This section should cover all the childcare routines and activities that are required to be undertaken in accordance with an agreed policy. Each

procedure should clearly indicate the minimum legal requirements as provided for within the nursery's registration, and the nursery's own standards
offer. The Childcare Act 2006 introduced a new, single framework for care
and education, the *Early Years Foundation Stage**, which brings together the
former, various regulatory reference points of *Birth to Three Matters**, the
Foundation Stage (of the National Curriculum) and the *National Standards
for Under 8s Daycare and Childminding**. This integrated standard endorses
the commitment of public policy makers to child-centred care and
education, and abolishes the divide between services offered in schools
(traditionally education) and others (traditionally perceived as offering care).

Another, surprisingly new, concept is that of children themselves
influencing what is provided. Although nurseries that follow the Italian
Reggio Emilia early years philosophy will be familiar with involving
children in the selection of activities and will have adopted an open-
ended approach to both the start and end of a project, preoccupation
with the raft of public policy measures in the last 10 years has precluded
much advance in practice in the UK. However, children's participation
is central to the *Every Child Matters** framework, and promotes children
as stakeholders in their own learning, and social and health care. In June
2006, Daycare Trust published *RAMPS: A Framework for Listening to Children**,
which outlines a practical way of empowering children to participate.
A typical contents list in this section would cover:

- Admission Policy
- Settling Children into the Nursery
- Staff Ratios and Qualifications
- Keyworking System
- Early Years' Curriculum
- Activity Planning and Evaluation
- Mounting and Display of Artwork
- Observation and Children's Profiles
- Total Service Quality Observation
- Child Discipline
- Meals
- Multi-Cultural Images
- Gender Policy
- Children with Special Needs
- Hygiene
- Health and Safety
- First Aid

- HIV and Hepatitis B
- Non-accidental injury (NAI)
- Child Protection
- Sick Children
- Children's Outings
- Collection of Children from the Nursery
- Relationship with Statutory Authorities and Local Community
- Relationship with Wider Community
- Visitors to the Nursery

An example of one of these procedures is given in Figure 2.5.

Staff care and development

The section on staff care would cover the following areas:

- terms and conditions of employment;
- equal opportunities;
- culture and behaviour
- work–life balance and well-being policy;
- staff recruitment procedures;
- induction training;
- training and development;
- supervision;
- staff appraisal;
- disciplinary procedures;
- grievance procedures;
- domestic/maintenance staff;
- students;
- volunteers.

An example of one of these procedures is given in Figure 2.6. A sample staff appraisal form is included as an appendix to this chapter.

Parent care and partnership

The parent care section should cover:

- partnership with parents;
- parent enquiries;
- showing parents around the nursery;
- parent contract;

MOUNTING AND DISPLAY OF ARTWORK

OBJECTIVE

To ensure display tables and mounted artwork are always presented attractively so that the children's work is the focal point.

PROCEDURE

When mounting artwork the display area should be defined by first backing the pinboard to highlight the area being used to display. Each individual piece of work should be backed at least once and when put up it should be symmetrical and in-line. Artwork should not be displayed at angles unless this enhances a project. Backing paper should always be in unobtrusive colours so that the focus is on the child's piece of work.

A child's picture should never be cut after completion and paper should never be pre-shaped in order to influence the child's creativity. The only exception however would be, for example, a shape project that was enhanced by the use of shaped paper. This method should be used cautiously.

Names should always be clearly printed in the left-hand corner so that the child understands the convention is left-to-right. Only the initial letter should be in capitals. If a child does not want his or her name on a piece of work the issue should not be forced and a compromise sought; i.e. 'Can I put your name on the back so as not to spoil your picture, then we will know it is yours?'

Handwriting should always be of a high standard and there should be no compromises on this issue. If there are good neat handwriters within the team others should be encouraged to use them. The company has a set of guidelines for letter formation which should be followed carefully. Each nursery agrees a universal alphabet so that each handwriter uses the same formation. Rulers should never be used by staff to keep print straight as they produce flat-bottomed letters.

Artwork should be replaced and refreshed regularly, and staples, BlueTack etc. should always be removed immediately. PrittStick and staples must not be used on walls. Unobtrusive methods of fixing should be used where possible; e.g. dress-making pins with a pin pusher.

Where appropriate, paper should be recycled (e.g. backing paper used more than once) for children's work.

Staples should be applied at an angle to ensure easy removal.

Paper should always be cut straight and a guillotine used to do this.

FIGURE 2.5 Example of a childcare and education procedure

STAFF APPRAISAL

OBJECTIVE

To ensure that staff receive regular and constructive feedback on their progress and that they have the opportunity to discuss privately any aspect of work or relationships that concerns them.

To redefine the professional development needs of the individual and to set out a programme for its fulfilment.

PROCEDURE

Staff are appraised at the end of their probationary period and then on a six-monthly basis in October and April.

The appraisal discussion takes place in private between the coordinator and member of staff and is based on the sections and headings of the appraisal form. Staff are notified at least five working days in advance of the date and time of their appraisal meeting and are given a copy of the appraisal form at that time to enable them to prepare for the meeting.

At the end of the appraisal meeting the appraisee is invited to enter any comments in the appropriate section of the form and to sign it.

All staff are entitled to have a copy of their appraisal if they so wish.

FIGURE 2.6 Example of a staff care and development procedure

- parent contact/meetings;
- involvement in nursery life;
- Nursery Steering Group/parent committee.

An example of a nursery steering group is given in Figure 2.7.

Accountability and records

The accountability section covers all areas of reporting for which the nursery manager is responsible. In some cases this will be information requested by the owner/company, and in others it will be prepared for the purposes of the Board or Steering Committee to which the manager reports. Certain reports are required by law, under the Children Act, and as inspected by OFSTED. These are Incident, Accident and Complaints reports, together with the Register of children.

Nursery Steering Group

PURPOSE

The Nursery Steering Group acts as a consultative body primarily to make recommendations for the further enhancement of the nursery services. The Group monitors standards, facilities and services provided, to ensure that they continue to be relevant to the needs of clients and in line with good practice.

MEMBERSHIP

The Group includes nursery management, parents, employer representatives and relevant local individuals who can bring influence and contribute to the continuous development of the nursery. The Group will include:

- Company Managing Director
- Company Operations Manager
- Nursery Manager
- One representative from each participating employer
- Two parent representatives.

It is desirable that the Group also includes:

- Nursery Deputy Manager
- One nominated local primary headteacher
- One representative from the local nursery training college
- One represenative from the participating developer, where relevant

TERMS OF REFERENCE

The Group will receive:

- A Nursery Manager's report, covering numbers of children, staff changes, and information on special projects/developments and staff training.
- A parent representatives' report, covering any issues received by the parent representatives that require discussion on nursery policy, i.e. those issues that cannot be resolved through the day-to-day practice of parent/nursery partnership.
- Items for discussion raised by the company representatives.

The above standard agenda items are intended to set the scene for ideas and discussion with respect to the ongoing development of the service provided by the nursery. The nursery management is also responsible for bringing to the notice of the Group any issues that may warrant discussion in the Group; these may include changes in legislation/public policy or company policy.

OPERATION

The Nursery Steering Group will meet every three months, i.e. four meetings each year. At least two weeks' notice should be given of meetings, which will normally be held at the nursery.

An Agenda will be drawn up by the Nursery Manager who will contact both parent and company representatives beforehand. The meetings will normally be chaired by the Manager, and will be minuted. Minutes will be posted on the Nursery Parents' Noticeboard and distributed to all members of the Group.

FIGURE 2.7 Nursery Steering Group

Other matters are orderly accounting and record-keeping, and form part of the properly run nursery's quality assurance package (see Chapter 7). The accountability section is likely to cover the following:

- children's applications for places;
- nursery places allocation and enrolment;
- reporting relationships;
- Nursery Management Board/Steering Group;
- children's records;
- staff records;
- local purchases and local repairs;
- financial administration;
- nursery income/expenditure reporting;
- incident reports;
- accident reports;
- staff planning;
- shift/rota planning;
- complaints;
- correspondence;
- filing.

An example of one of these procedures is given in Figure 2.8.

Nursery maintenance

Alongside the growth in the private nursery sector during the last ten years has been the recognition of the part played by a good environment for childhood. Most nurseries are now run in purpose-built or specially converted buildings. The Rumbold report (1990)* said that 'Educators and their architects need to ensure that the learning environment both inside and out is well designed and organised so as to be accessible, comprehensible and stimulating for the children; that equipment is appropriate and in satisfactory condition; and that the best use is made of the particular opportunities offered by the locality'. It is equally important to ensure that the nursery layout facilitates supervision of children, and is flexible to the changing day-by-day space needs. Children and staff need to feel secure in their environment, and staff do not want to use precious time on 'policing' different corners of the nursery, rather than interacting with children in a focused and undistracted way. Equally children and staff like to redefine their space, to suit the needs of the group utilising the

---

INCIDENT REPORTS

OBJECTIVE

To establish an accurate record of any incident that occurs at the nursery or to any member of staff or child in nursery operating time, which may need to be recounted at a later date.

PROCEDURE

On being informed of an incident that needs to be recorded, the Coordinator should immediately gain as much information as possible. The incident form should be completed immediately.

The Coordinator should then use his/her discretion about reporting the incident immediately to Head Office. This should be done for any event requiring communication to any external body/individual.

At all times the parents/carers should be informed of any incident and a copy of the form offered to them.

FIGURE 2.8 An example of an accountability and records procedure

particular area of the nursery, to create a fresh arrangement, to juxtapose activity areas in better ways.

The nursery environment is critical to the performance of the service and this section of the manual will reflect your concern with that aspect.

Clearly the relationship between the nurture of positive attitudes towards the nursery environment and health and safety is close. But it is also about making life easier for staff, so that they can concentrate on what they are uniquely capable of doing, and developing children's attitudes towards space, property and respect for what other people are doing. The contents list in this section may cover:

- nursery design and layout;
- opening and closing procedures;
- cleaning;
- equipment servicing;
- building repairs and equipment repair/replacement;
- housekeeping standards;
- fire drill;
- crime prevention.

An example of one of these procedures is given in Figure 2.9.

CLEANING

OBJECTIVE

To ensure that the nursery is maintained to the highest standards of cleanliness and hygiene.

PROCEDURES

The general cleaning of the nursery should take place out of operating hours, either in the early morning or after the nursery closes at night. Daily cleaning must include the following:

- sweeping of external paths and patio areas
- cleaning/vacuuming of entrance lobby
- mopping of floor
- dusting of display surfaces and ledges and cleaning of work/play surfaces
- thorough cleaning of toilets, wash basins, mirrors and of kitchen equipment and surfaces.

Windows should be cleaned monthly though it may be necessary for some windows to be cleaned more frequently.

It is the responsibility of nursery staff during the day to ensure that the nursery is constantly maintained in a clean and hygienic condition. Accidents and spills must be attended to immediately and the kitchen and other food areas should be thoroughly cleaned after food preparation and meals.

FIGURE 2.9 An example of a nursery maintenance procedure

Emergency procedures

This is the last, but by no means least important, section of any nursery manual. The procedures here need to be unequivocally clear and cover all possible eventualities. By their very nature, they will need to be read, absorbed, rehearsed and acted upon quickly and smoothly. They also combine the absolute minimum in terms of procedures that each and every individual member of staff, however temporary, should be aware of.

Clearly in this section it is *vital* to maintain current telephone numbers, nominated individuals, authorities, etc.

Certain emergency procedures should be displayed, usually as bullet-point instructions, as well as comprising part of the reference manual. They are basic health and safety precautions and will be required to be in place not only as part of the nursery registration, but also as an essential prerequisite of insurance policies relating to children, staff, visitors and premises. The contents in this section of the manual should cover as a minimum:

- fire;
- break-in;
- theft;
- power cut;
- bomb scare;
- accident;
- illness;
- failure to collect a child.

An example of one of these procedures is given in Figure 2.10.

Appendices

The comprehensive nursery manual will have a number of appendices. These may include reference points, such as a copy of the registration document, current public policy documents, such as *Every Child Matters**, recognised quality indicators, such as the EPPE* study summary, and the *Early Years Foundation Stage** curriculum. It may also include a pack of standard letters/documentation used with parents and with staff. It can also include a full set of sample children's records documentation. Anything not included, but used in a standard format, should be clearly referenced as part of expected practice and daily use.

FIRE EMERGENCY PROCEDURE

If you discover fire (and cannot put it out at once), raise the alarm immediately.

The Coordinator/Deputy is responsible for telephoning the fire brigade and Head Office. In their absence the most senior person on duty has the responsibility.

The Coordinator or Deputy should check that the building is empty of children, staff and other visitors. Close the doors and windows, if it is safe to do so, and then leave the building by the nearest exit. If it has not yet been collected, they should take the attendance form as they leave.

In the event of a fire breaking out in the kitchen, the cook should if possible turn off electrical and gas appliances before leaving.

Once outside, all occupants of the nursery should go straight to the assembly point under the chestnut tree in front of the office building. The Coordinator/Deputy will then use the attendance form to check that everyone is safe.

FIGURE 2.10 An example of an emergency procedure

APPENDIX TO CHAPTER 2

Appraisal Form: Nursery Officer

Name ....

Position ....

Date of appointment ....

Date of appraisal ....

Introduction to the Appraisal Form

1. The purpose of this form is to assist the appraiser and appraisee reach agreement in evaluating job performance and then determining what further help or training is needed for career development.

2. The form is in four parts:

    PART ONE   Measures performance in relation to the agreed responsibilities and accountabilities set out in the job description.

    PART TWO   Measures performance in relation to the personal qualities or skills that are agreed to be most appropriate to the requirements of the job.

    PART THREE   Provides space for the appraiser to record the action or further assistance needed to enable the appraisee to improve job performance and achieve career progression.

    Part Four   Provides space for the appraisee to enter any comments that he or she wishes to make.

3. In PARTS ONE and TWO, the appraiser and appraisee need to agree a performance rating for the responsibility, personal quality or skill under discussion. The scale is as follows:

    5   Excellent quality
    4   Very good
    3   Expected competency
    2   Poor – considerable scope for improvement
    1   Very weak – major improvement required urgently

    Entries in PART ONE (reproduced here) relate to the job being performed and not necessarily to the person carrying out the job. For example, if the appraisee is new to the position, the rating will not necessarily reflect the contribution of the appraisee. However, if the appraisee has held the position for a long time, the ratings will reflect on the person and the job.

4. In all cases the appraisee should receive a copy of this form at least one week before the appraisal meeting and be asked to complete PARTS ONE and TWO in readiness for the discussion.

    The appraiser will also complete PARTS ONE and TWO.

    The meeting itself will then seek consensus on the performance ratings and the action and assistance needed.

    PART FOUR is for the appraisee to enter any comments on the appraisal.

PART ONE: RESPONSIBILITIES AND ACCOUNTABILITIES

Enter below the appraisee's key responsibilities from the job description.

KEY RESPONSIBILITIES	RATING
1. *To ensure that the children are cared for in a happy stimulating environment following the principles of childcare embodied in the company's Nursery Manual.*	
• familiarity, acceptance and demonstrations of expectations and philosophies stated in the manual	
• contribution to the creation and maintenance of a stimulating and challenging environment for the children	
• ability to make appropriate and efficient use of teaching space	
• ability to devise relevant and interesting activities and experiences	
• ability to use stimulating resources	
• ability to plan a suitable range and balance of activity	
• consistency of mood-friendliness, warmth and good nature at all times	
2. *To ensure that the developmental needs of children are met within a framework of planned activity that also enables learning to take place within an anti-racist and non-sexist environment.*	
• provision of activities to match current learning needs of children	
• ability to respond appropriately to the initiatives demonstrated by the children	
• awareness of the potential learning opportunities embodied within the range of activities	
• ability to focus children's attention and maximise upon learning opportunities	
• ability to modify teaching in the light of individual responses	
• ability to make the most of young children's curiosity	
• awareness of the need to encourage equal opportunities, e.g. boys in the home corner, girls in the bricks	
• demonstration that all children and cultures are valued as common practice	
• to maximise opportunities to promote the positive benefits of living in a pluralistic society	
• provision of opportunities for first-hand experimentation, exploration, observation, discussion and investigation	
NOTES:	

KEY RESPONSIBILITIES	RATING
3. *To ensure that high standards of hygiene and safety are maintained at all times and that the policies and procedures of the nursery are correctly followed.*	
• establishment of good working relationships with the children	
• calmness and manner of dealing with difficult situations/behaviour	
• ability to redirect children when necessary	
• ability to organise and direct the children	
• ability safely to organise and maintain materials and equipment in both short and long term	
• ability to anticipate potentially unsafe or disruptive situations and divert	
• compliance with expected health and safety routines, e.g. hand-washing, kitchen vigilance, first aid, fire drills, general safety awareness	
• ability to exude a sense of security by having clear expectations and defining boundaries to children	
• being supportive of other staff and presenting a united approach	
• ability to ensure that activities taking place at the same time are compatible	
• ability to manage own activity while keeping an overview of the rest of the activities in the nursery	
• awareness of other children in the nursery when engaged with own group	
4. *To keep careful observations of the children within the keyworker role, building up a full profile of each through close liaison with other agencies, supporting staff concerned with each child, and meaningful and regular dialogue with parents or carers.*	
• ability to form effective warm relationships with children	
• willingness and ability to make contact with parents	
• openness to creating links with other agencies	
• initiating and maintaining dialogue with other staff members	
• ability to talk knowledgeably about given children	
• ability to keep meaningful notes	
• ability to observe children and recognise what is meaningful to them	
• ability to intervene appropriately in children's activities	
• ability to make an assessment of each child's needs	
• assessing quality of the relationship with parents and recognising when there is strain	
NOTES:	

KEY RESPONSIBILITIES	RATING
5. *To cooperate and communicate with the Coordinator and Deputy on all nursery matters, contribute to staff meetings, participate as a responsible member of the team, and present a professional code of conduct at all times.*	
• appearance – attitude – speech	
• punctuality	
• reliability	
• vitality	
• sensitivity to situations	
• ability to identify own strengths and weaknesses and complement other team members/training	
• willingness to ask for and act upon advice	
• willingness to develop a rapport and good professional relationships with staff	
• contribute to staff meetings/participate as a responsible member of the team and any other occasions when representing the company	
• willingness to attend conferences/meetings etc.	
NOTES:	

COMMENTS FROM APPRAISER
PERFORMANCE:
CAREER DEVELOPMENT PLAN:
Signed .... (appraisee)
Date ....

Chapter 3

Leading a team and managing a service

- Motivation and commitment
- Roles and responsibilities
- Teamwork
- The team manager
- Dealing with conflicts
- Selling the nursery
- Working to a plan
- Furthering the quality of service
- Planning staff shifts
- Communication
- Personal well-being
- Managing yourself and others
- Understanding behaviours
- Appendix

MOTIVATION AND COMMITMENT

Neither a lofty degree of intelligence nor imagination nor both together go to the making of a genius. Love, love, love, that is the soul of a genius.

Mozart

There has been much written about the personal and professional attributes of those providing non-parental care and education of young children, which has drawn a great deal of public attention, particularly in the residential care sector. Researchers in the pre-school field have consistently drawn attention to the low status or reward predicament of nursery nurses and teachers. Whitebook *et al.* (1989)* and others highlighted the influence of staff disaffection and turnover on children's social and language development; Penn (1994)* identified direct links between parent satisfaction with services, and conditions of employment. Guidance to the Children Act issued by the Department of Health recognises this research to the extent that it draws attention to the rights of people working with young children. Similarly, Angela Rumbold (1990)* said that:

The status afforded to any group or profession has an important influence on the recognition and support it secures for itself. Yet adults working with under fives have traditionally enjoyed less esteem than

53

those working with children of statutory school age, outside and even within the ranks of the professions themselves. This is reflected in substantial measure, in terms of pay, moreover differences of relative status between groups concerned with the under fives go beyond those inherent in, or flowing or receiving from, their different level of training. Besides coming within different sets of arrangements for pay and conditions of service, the groups differ markedly in their opportunities for in-service training – though all alike suffer limitations in their career prospects.

It is noteworthy that one of the imperatives that has been a driving force behind the establishment of many independent sector nurseries is the need for employers to retain staff. Yet how effective are we at this very aspect of management? Not very effective, according to Penn.

Until now, there have been a number of training routes towards working with under-fives: the traditional, formal, college-based qualification route, and the system of accreditation of competency introduced in 1991 through National Vocational Qualifications (NVQs). As NVQ candidates have been assessed in their own workplace, there have been issues with achieving a consistent standard on which all employers can rely. There has also been an ongoing debate as to whether NVQ2, or NVQ3 should be seen as 'qualified'.

With the publication of the Labour Government's *Ten Year Strategy for Childcare**, a new body was formed to look at the whole children's workforce, the Children's Workforce Development Council (CWDC). In August 2006, CWDC published its approach to the creation of, and the standards it would be looking for, in a new qualification, the Early Years Professional Status (EYPS), which responded directly to the EPPE* finding that the leader of a setting was critical to improving outcomes for children. Proposals have been consulted on widely, and have been broadly welcomed. The central aim of this integrated approach to training for and qualifying for work with children is to improve outcomes for children. The EYPS prospectus identifies four principal challenges for the sector:

- recruiting more people into the children's workforce;
- developing and retaining more people in the workforce;
- strengthening integrated working and developing new workforce roles;
- improving and strengthening leadership, management and supervision.

A 'Transformation Fund' was launched at the same time to improve the quality of provision through training the existing workforce to EYPS level, without passing on the cost to parents. The Government's aim is to have EYPS in all Children's Centres by 2010, and in every setting by 2015. Not everyone in a setting will have EYPS; however, neither is it intended that EYPS is necessarily adequate for the leader of the setting, particularly if it offers integrated services. It is clear that both the EYPS candidate's experience and previous qualifications should be taken into account when considering the appropriate training pathway. Before embarking on EYPS accreditation, the candidate will need to achieve at NVQ Level 6, i.e. a degree, or hold an Early Years Foundation Degree (Level 5). Over time, CWDC is committed to looking at pathways to EYPS for those holding Level 3 qualifications coupled with significant experience. This is being developed in 2007 through the Integrated Qualifications Framework (IQF), which is being designed to consolidate the numerous qualifications that currently exist across all children's services, not just early years. While the remit of the CWDC is to bring together and simplify the range of qualifications available, its structure is designed to be more accessible to employers, so they can better identify the appropriately qualified person for the vacancy they are filling. IQF will be comprised of eight levels, up to and including higher education professional qualifications, such as those already discussed.

Although it is not expected that all those working in the *Early Years Foundation Stage** will hold EYPS, it is clear that the qualification bar is going up for those working with children. In *Building an Integrated Workforce for a Long term Vision of Universal Early Education and Care*, (Daycare Trust 2004), it was considered that unless 60 per cent of the workforce was qualified to degree level then agreed aspirations of quality would not be achieved. EPPE* evidenced the key factors contributing to the quality of experience and outcomes for children as residing in the quality of leaders and those trained to teacher/equivalent level working alongside less qualified staff. There is also substantial support for the idea that the single biggest difference in young children's emotional development could be achieved through peer support and teamwork. Building a strong nursery team for the future will require a commitment to such expectations. Given that 40 per cent of the workforce is not qualified to 'A' level standard (Daycare Trust 2005), the most immediate issue is probably to lift English and maths skills within the existing workforce.

If we look at the make-up of the early years workforce now, using the *Labour Force Survey* (2001–2003) it is characterised by being:

- mostly female (86–98 per cent);
- mostly from white ethnic backgrounds (96–98 per cent);
- mostly young;
- mostly less qualified than teachers.

What might this look like in a few years' time, post-EYPS, and how can we prepare ourselves for this? Interestingly, the Working Families' Employer of the Year Award winner who was mentioned earlier is now having to consider providing childcare as a work–life offer to staff, because it has been so successful at retaining graduates – the organisation's long-term attrition point. With more years of training behind this group, the workforce is likely to reach, for instance, child-bearing age. This will present a new set of challenges to the early years sector.

The emphasis that is placed on training and development post qualification simply reflects the fact that the delivery of nursery services does not stand still. Both regulators and parents expect more, and every day we learn more about the entitlements of children. Updating original and fundamental skills and acquiring new knowledge are the parallel lines of in-service training. The leaders' responsibility is to anticipate and identify what is needed by those who use the service, and to provide it.

This will include recognising that one of the few aspects of early years' service provision that all commentators seem to agree on is that quality of service, in large measure, depends on continuity in the staff team. How can we attract good staff in the first place and encourage commitment? A recent conversation I had with a human resources adviser in a national nursery group revealed that what staff who stay value most is that they are listened to, that their experience and contribution is valued and recognised, and that it is understood they can accept responsibility. They want their differences respected and they seek support through change. Only after this did salary begin to feature. If we know this, why do we not include the way we respond to these priorities within job adverts? Nothing in my experience has led me to believe that staff do not understand the basic economics of the profession they are entering or that they leave a post for salary reasons alone – provided the salary structure is transparent and fair. The same human resources advisor told me that retention could be enhanced by adopting the same approach as we do with children: 'Why don't we use our childcare knowledge of what brings out the best in children, and use it with our staff? Praise what they do well, recognise their achievements and key into their interests.'

Ironically, the introduction of EYPS as equivalent to teacher status but without a similar commitment to raise salaries for senior nursery staff could change nursery staff's view of what they are paid. Alternatively, it may encourage more to become teachers in schools rather than stay within the nursery sector.

Regular, anonymous surveys amongst staff can help to inform management of the main barriers to successful retention of staff; however, nothing can replace personal contact with people who themselves are 'people people' and tuning into the way they see their role, their work and the conditions under which they are expected to practise their professional skills and perform.

Having moved on from the embryonic sector-development stage of owning and managing a nursery, an increasing number of nurseries now either belong to a group or have formed a collaboration with another childcare provider, e.g. a school, local authority or voluntary organisation. This is good news for staff, who are more likely to find promotion opportunities within the organisation they are currently with. It will increase the scope for planned career development and retention for employers, and help to maintain their investment in recruitment and training. It will also help to lift salaries and the professional status of nursery staff, as competition for staff is placed on a more level playing field.

But although every nursery hopes to keep its good people, it must also survive financially. It is not possible simply to go on paying people more money for doing the same job, even though they may be doing it better or more efficiently and bringing more experience to bear. The nursery manager has to employ more subtle means than pay, to sustain commitment. My own staff's priority list suggested that, in any event, salary is not the only or even the most highly-rated reward that nursery staff seek.

The importance of understanding, sharing in and contributing to nursery philosophy is dealt with in Chapter 5. Suffice it to say here, that belonging to 'a team' and making a long-term commitment means being able to sign up to the team's objectives, working with – not despite – the flow. It relates to inclusion (Chapter 1) and being involved in change (Chapter 7).

It is reasonable that nursery staff should expect to work in an environment that allows them to practise the skills and knowledge they have acquired. Skills and knowledge will go on developing, but without an equivalent development in the way space is arranged, or material resources chosen and sourced, staff will be limited in their ability to put their plans into action. Without doubt this will lead to professional frustration.

ROLES AND RESPONSIBILITIES

A nursery is not like an office. Whereas office workers can settle in each morning, with a coffee or a chat, or even get stuck straight into writing, making telephone calls or a business meeting, it is not an option for nursery staff to put people off until they feel ready for the conversation. Children and parents rely on the nursery to have a routine, which is not adjustable to suit staff preferences or personal priorities. Upholding a routine requires each and every individual staff team member to know what is expected of them at all points in the day: what and who they are responsible for; where they are based in the nursery; and which tasks are to be completed. If there is any room for misunderstanding in any aspects of this, then child, parent and colleague are let down.

But a nursery team is not a regiment, and neither should a good nursery feel like an institution. The planning and processes that allow the nursery to function smoothly should not be allowed to overpower the objective of offering the blend of warmth and professionalism that we all seek.

Goldschmied and Jackson (1994)* warn us against the takeover of 'institutional rush'. This is where the important aspect or phase of an activity or period in a day is overwhelmed by the need to prepare for the next activity or period. Goldschmied and Jackson cite the example of a lunchtime they observed, where there was a harmful and disturbing sense that the meal had to be got over with. This was traced to the fact that the staff who washed up had a contract, which meant they had to finish by 1 p.m. This deadline had a ripple effect back to the moment when the children sat down at their tables. How much social interaction was lost, and how much sheer pleasure in the meal was forgone by children and staff?

For a manager, defining roles and responsibilities focuses on the following challenges:

- How can we ensure that 'institutional rush' does not take over?
- How can we ensure that the nursery runs smoothly, and that there is time for play and rest?
- How can we ensure that one activity runs smoothly into another, to reduce the incidence of children roaming in an unfocused way?

- How can we ensure that each member of the team knows how to bring the best out in each other and understands the importance of teamwork?

There is a hierarchy of traditional personnel tools available to promote understanding of individual responsibilities, and of how these fit into the overall scheme for roles within an organisation. They form the building blocks for staff to know whether or not they are getting their roles right. The most important components are the job description, the induction programme, and staff appraisal (see the appendix to Chapter 2). These standard components should be drawn up, having considered the breakdown of responsibilities that need to be covered by nursery staff (see Figure 3.1).

Children-related responsibilities:

- programme of activities
- care routines
- maintaining occupancy

Staff-related responsibilities:

- recruitment and employment
- support and direction
- deployment and teamwork
- development and training

Parent-related responsibilities:

- liaison and contracts
- participation and partnership
- feedback

Organisation-related responsibilities:

- finance
- administration
- marketing

Outside responsibilities:

- registration and inspection
- liaison with related professions, e.g. health, education
- local community

FIGURE 3.1 Breakdown of responsibilities

Many of the areas of responsibility listed in Figure 3.1 are dealt with in some detail in other chapters of the book. Here I would like to focus on those important management issues that arise over and over again in daily practice, and principally relate to people working well, or not so well, together.

You might say that the list of responsibilities may equally apply to a good nursery nurse as to a nursery manager, particularly as far as the first three categories in Figure 3.1 are concerned. However, the comment would not be inconsistent with the central theme of this book that managerial responsibility should be totally integrated into the professional role. When accepting the job as manager, you do not go through a metamorphosis and leave behind you everything you know and the way you approach your core discipline of nursery nursing or teaching. On the contrary, you have been selected because of your abilities in these areas, to develop your experience of managing others in those more specialist roles.

No-one can be a leader if they don't have followers! The functions of leadership, over and above the management role, were discussed in Chapter 1. A reference was made to 'leader-ful teams' where all staff can be a leader by accepting real responsibility for an area of work. Staff need to feel empowered to accept leadership, and they will need to be provided with the skills and confidence and authority to act as leaders. This is why many nurseries have difficulty with the title of 'manager' or 'director', and prefer 'coordinator' or 'head of Centre' – terms that imply the existence of a team. In addition to the concept of leader-ful teams, Pen Green Research Centre has developed the notion of 'guardianship'. This is where each senior member of staff takes responsibility for a particular 'domain'. This includes day-to-day responsibility for the service offered, but it is recognised that the needs of the local community in relation to the service must be understood, respected and responded to. The domain guardian engages in public policy that influences and impacts on their domain, and becomes a passionate advocate for their area of work. Domains may be a particular service, e.g. 0–3 provision or after-school services, or it might be a virtual domain, such as pedagogy or involving parents in their children's learning. Asking staff to choose their domain can help them get back in touch with their real passion for working with children – so frequently forgotten in the face of 'institutional rush'.

TEAMWORK

Nursery services involve a number of sets of people, their relationships, and their feelings. Managing these relies on the subordination of individual interests and needs in order jointly to provide coordinated activities to achieve common purposes. This is why teamwork is important.

No nursery would wish to think that it has anything but an open and welcoming atmosphere. Achieving this has much to do with the outlook of staff and fulfilment in their posts. The basic requirements for working well together are:

- shared aims and objectives;
- a common working language;
- the ability to manage relationships as well as tasks.

Setting out the aims and objectives of the nursery as a whole is discussed in Chapter 6 in some detail. In order that each individual can feel valued and take personal responsibility for the quality of their contribution, they must know where and for what, together and jointly, the staff team is aiming. To exclude a team member from acquiring this is both demeaning and demoralising, and undermines the knowledge and experience they bring with them to their job.

In discussion of aims and objectives, it is equally important that no member of the team feels excluded because of the principles on which the aims and objectives are based. I am referring here to basic assumptions and attitudes towards children and parents, equal opportunities and work.

Ground rules need to be established in order that all staff feel they belong to the team equally, and the manager needs to role model such behaviour and culture as the nursery wishes to foster. Ben Zander, in *The Art of Possibility* (2000)*, describes how effective it is to separate a person's or group's contribution from its achievement. Contribution becomes valuable in itself, and does not lead to inevitable comparison. Thinking of oneself as a contribution shifts us away from self-concern and towards a relationship with others that is focused on making a difference together. Offering others the opportunity to contribute is then a revolutionary way of bringing a team together. Everyone gets a chance to lead practice, even though they are not the leader of the team. Everyone should be empowered to bring forward an idea, to craft a proposal to put the idea into practice, to have the proposal assessed and approved, to be invited to develop it, and to celebrate the outcome.

To a significant extent, the 'health' of a nursery relies on the quality of relationships developed within the team. This is an important area for the manager's attention, particularly when a new member joins. There is another reason to focus on this area, and that is ensuring that all members of the team are comfortable with raising a difficult issue concerning a peer. In 2005 a BBC undercover exposé of poor practice in some nurseries highlighted a child's experience of being ignored and verbally abused in a nursery. At no point was there only one member of staff in the room; however, those not directly involved did not feel empowered to come forward and speak with the manager. Allowing poor practice to continue unchecked breeds complacency and laziness and changes the culture of the nursery. Team spirit and collegiality is a crucial plank of good practice, and the standards we set ourselves in this respect are more important to parents than the minimums required of us by regulators.

The way we behave towards each other, to allow everyone to reach their full potential and belong to the team, are complex concepts that need to be explained and understood. The very best example I have seen comes from Bright Horizons Family Solutions. The Heart Principles are in poster form in every one of the company's nurseries, and form part of staff induction (see Figure 3.2).

As a member of a team, you will have certain responsibilities assigned to you that will involve a number of tasks to be accomplished. As a manager, many of your tasks will be to ensure that others fulfil their responsibilities appropriately. Ensuring that somebody does something involves not only making sure that the task is understood, but that the individual is willing and able to undertake it. The manager is then concerned with the relationship of one member of staff to another, and how the delegation of tasks and deployment of staff affects them as people. An individual may be the right person to do something, but someone else may be making it difficult in some way for that task to be carried out. The manager needs to unblock this situation.

Teamwork recognises a current belief in the value of *management by participation* – working together as equal members of a team provides social support that relieves the strain and stress of nursery life. Group morale can be influenced for better or worse by the disposition of any one member.

But the 'team leader', the nursery manager, is still held responsible for the achievements and failures of a team. The nursery manager is responsible for taking the team from birth to maturity (Rodd, 1994)*.

FIGURE 3.2 *(facing page)* Bright Horizons Family Solutions: The Heart Principles

Mission Statement

The Bright Horizons Family Solutions mission is to provide innovative programmes that
help children, families, and employers work together to be their very best.
We are committed to providing the highest quality child care,
early education, and work/life solutions in the world.

WE STRIVE TO:

Nurture each child's unique qualities and potential

Support families through strong partnerships

Collaborate with employers to build family-friendly workplaces

Create a work environment that encourages professionalism, growth, and diversity

Grow a financially strong organisation

We aspire to do this so successfully that we make a difference in the lives of
children and families and in the communities where we live and work.

Bright Horizons
FAMILY SOLUTIONS

Honesty Excellence Accountability Respect Teamwork

HEART
Principles

Bright Horizons
FAMILY SOLUTIONS

HEART

Bright Horizons mission
provide innovative
grammes that help children,
ies, and employers work
ther to be their very best.
one of us has an important
o play in fulfilling that
on. We care passionately
, what we do, and we are
mitted to building an
isation that will make a
ence for generations to
. Many will come after us
mplete the work we have
. Our HEART principles
guide to help us support
nother and reflect the spirit
company in the important
that we do each day.

HONESTY   EXCELLENCE   ACCOUNTABILITY   RESPECT   TEAMWORK

- **Communication is at the heart of all we do.** We are engaged in the moment, giving each child, parent, colleague, or client our full attention.

- **We give explanations, not orders.** As we lead and inspire, we use every opportunity to teach, not just tell.

- **We value input from our colleagues.** We are interested in and respect the opinions of those with whom we work — we want to know what others think.

- **We celebrate and encourage the diversity of adults in our community in the same way we cherish and respect the individuality of the children in our care.** We strengthen our organisation by embracing diversity and never allowing acts of non-acceptance.

- **We create an atmosphere of honesty and trust by openly communicating with one another.** We resolve our conflicts within the Bright Horizons family. When we are upset with an individual we do not complain to others; we have the courage to speak to the subject of our concern.

- **We are accountable for our actions.** We admit and learn from our mistakes; we do not dwell on them.

- **As leaders in our field, we are committed to continuous learning and improvement.** We challenge ourselves to ask questions, seek solutions, and embrace new ideas.

- **We are problem-solvers, not problem-dodgers.** Whoever receives a question or concern owns it until it is resolved. When the dirty nappy hits the fan, some people run for cover; we break out the cleaning supplies.

- **We ask the question, "Why not?"** before we say "no" to employees, parents, and clients, with the understanding that an unconditional "yes" is not always an appropriate answer.

- **Our clients and families of children in our care count on us.** We listen to their needs and concerns and then respond with a sense of urgency.

- **"Quality" is a description we earn and maintain every day by attending carefully to the small tasks.** Quality carries through to how we perform, how we present ourselves, how we maintain our facilities, and how we rally together as a team to respond to new challenges.

- **We cannot afford to develop solutions that cause us to be profitable at the expense of quality, nor can we afford to have quality at the expense of profit.** Profit is our oxygen line, a life-giving element without which we could not continue to fulfill our mission.

- **Growth is our security.** To sustain our growth, people must also grow professionally. We embrace new ideas and are committed to developing our future leaders.

- **We recognise each other's efforts in achieving our goals and find ways to celebrate our successes.** We consider each other's contributions, time, and feelings by acknowledging each other and saying, "thank you."

- **We are doing serious and important work.** We take pride in what we do, and we must never lose sight of the joy and fun in our work.

Getting together

The first stage of the development of a team is when a group of people become aware that they are going to be working together. The clock in Figure 3.3 illustrates the ensuing phases in the development. Even though a team may feel it has reached the third or even fourth quarter, a new joiner or a leaver will push the clock back, and the development process will need to start 'ticking' again. Whenever the team's composition changes, the start of a 'new' team is signalled. Existing staff will have anxieties about a new member's competence; a new member will need to learn how to belong – the ground rules.

As manager you need to facilitate this 'forming' process by providing opportunities for personal and professional getting-to-know sessions, for example a meal before a staff meeting. You need to be available and accessible, not judgemental, and observing of the ways in which staff are interacting. This will build trust and security among team members. The next step for them is to start to take risks and to challenge each other.

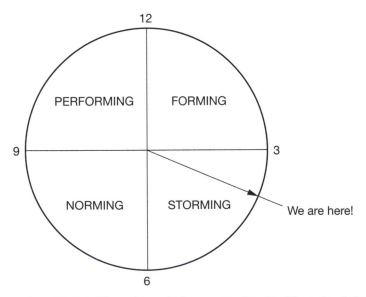

FIGURE 3.3 The ticking clock representing the life cycle of the team

Confronting conflict

After an initial 'honeymoon' period, it is natural for team members to start asserting themselves, to start negotiating rotas and responsibilities according to their skills and interests. People become concerned with procedures, policies and who sets the agenda, and question decision-making procedures. 'I only take instructions from the manager' and 'They can't tell us to do that' start to typify discussion.

Respect for each individual's contribution, and support in equal measure demonstrated through informal supervision and formal appraisal, are critical to this stage of team building, and time must be put aside by the manager to ensure that they are provided.

Conflict is inevitable in a group, and it leads to healthy discussion and positive solutions, when effectively managed. This is 'storming'. If conflict is avoided, then discussions are put off, leaving everyone feeling frustrated and low. Above all, staff will probably be reluctant to attend and contribute to further meetings.

The manager's skill here is to be an active listener, and to be an assertive chairperson – to ensure that everyone has their say, but that the discussion is moved on. Time should be taken at the outset of the meeting to provide up-to-date information and to clarify expectations of the meeting, in order that discussion remains focused. If staff are able to vent irrelevant frustrations, they only hold up the meeting, and leave feeling bad about using the meeting for that purpose. Such an issue needs to be identified and time set aside elsewhere to deal with it.

Consensus and cooperation

Having worked through some conflict, members of the team are probably now ready and need to experiment with new practices, engage in open debate, and challenge long-standing procedures. This is because members now trust each other, and value the results of working as a combined unit.

Reaching this stage heralds the advent of change. 'We' is heard more often that 'I' or 'You'. Conflicts may still occur but the members now wish to protect group cohesion, and it will be overcome positively.

The manager's role here is to promote cohesion by involving staff in goal-setting and the development of policy, enabling staff to implement new practices themselves. Then team spirit has been engendered and the process of 'norming' has begun.

Effective team performance

Now all members are making an equal, and equally valued, contribution to the task. Change is anticipated and planned for, and the team embraces it as a new challenge. The team becomes proud of its achievements, and members reacquire their independence as well as their interdependence (see Case Study 4).

The manager is able to relax, and turn his or her attention to the development of other future leaders, to 'Where do we want to go next' in terms of service development. But this phase of team development will last only until a member leaves or a new member joins, and the clock starts to tick again. The manager must be sensitive to the needs of others at this point: This wouldn't have happened if Lorraine was still here', and 'Wasn't it great before all the changes', need to be accepted as part of the process, and worked through in order that the team moves forward again.

When there is a wholesale change in the team, most members will remember how good the team-building process felt and will be highly motivated to reach effective team performance again.

THE TEAM MANAGER

On a daily basis, a manager moves from being an administrator to being in direct care of children, and back again. Both manager and team members must adapt to the constant changes in a manager's position in the team.

When in the office, the manager's role can be understood; when she is working directly with children, is she the person in authority? How should team members interact with the manager when she is working with children?

If the team has reached a stage of effective performance, the presence of the manager as one of the team should not present a problem: there is a shared respect and task goals are clear. However, when others in the team are still trying to establish their authority, demonstrate their contribution, fulfil their role, then the manager's presence can cause confusion.

However, the manager's participation in day-to-day interactions should not be avoided. It is important to remember that the nursery exists firstly for children, and secondly for parents – both of whom need to see and know the manager.

Some ways in which the manager can add to the performance of the team and stay true to the roles and responsibilities already established are:

Case Study 4

Nursery teams were asked to look at how they would move around the clock more effectively, and to set themselves a 'challenge'; here are two different approaches:

Nursery A's team challenge is 'communication'. This will entail the following:

- Listen to one another and allow each staff member to have their say.
- Appreciate one another's opinions and value any relevant information that is being passed on.
- Learn to compromise in the event of disagreement.
- Be more open about criticism. If there is a problem, address the staff member in question and avoid discussing the matter when the person is not there.

Nursery B's team challenge is:

- to improve communication within the nursery, particularly between the two areas – upstairs and downstairs – we believe that this will provide increased opportunities for new experiences and self-development for both staff and children;
- to work towards increased organisation in the maintenance of the nursery without compromising the care or stimulation of the children; to streamline the 'chores' and encourage people to take joint responsibility for these duties by way of rotas and job lists – the aim is to be constantly reviewing and improving the nursery and increased respect for our environment;
- to increase confidence and to support one another in activity planning; to build up resources and establish an index and storage system that enables staff to access resources when needed; to maximise opportunities for new ideas and a wide variety of activities so that staff and children are involved in a fresh and interesting programme each day;
- to increase our liaison with other nurseries within the company by way of visits and officer meetings;
- to learn more about the community in which we are sited and to build on the relationships with that community.

- to act as a role model through interacting with children, parents and staff in a professional and authoritative manner;
- to introduce a new activity or new resources, i.e. extend the programme for children;
- to use the time as a training session for a new member of the team.

Equally, to avoid the following would be wise:

- undertaking spot checks on procedures whilst participating;
- automatically taking over a child who is having problems settling;
- intervening in a key-worker–parent dialogue before being asked.

The features of a good team are that it: shares a consistent approach to problems, allows time for its members to participate, and has a system for evaluating progress in dealing with tasks. The manager of a team pulls all this together, and coordinates the work.

Since the aim is to provide a consistent service that is capable of withstanding staff absences, embracing different levels of experience, and coping with the similar problems of different parents and children, the manager needs to be able to rely on staff to deal with matters in a way that is based on common policies and procedures. No one individual can be at a nursery for the full extent of its opening hours, which inevitably leads to a number of staff members dealing with any particular issue. As we have already seen, committing standard procedures to writing can facilitate consistency. Feedback, discussion and review, with the manager acting as coordinator, can take it still further.

This means making time for such dialogue. The manager will need to assess whether immediate support for a staff member or situation is required; or whether the necessary follow-up can take place at the next staff meeting.

In order to move forward together, it is important that as a whole the staff team have the opportunity to share experiences: to consider whether they can all adopt the same approach when faced with a similar situation, and whether a new or revised procedure should be incorporated into the nursery manual. Making time to reflect on nursery practice together is key to moving forward at a pace that keeps up with children's entitlements and parents' expectations. The nursery day is full of details, interruptions, snatched conversations, emergencies, responsive actions. In order to think together, time needs to be reserved, preferably not when the team is tired or at the end of the week.

I referred earlier to the role of a nursery manager being that of a coordinator. My managers were called coordinators because of the emphasis we placed on teamwork, and its close relationship to quality of service. In the role of a team leader a manager is required to:

- respond to others' needs;
- promote team 'spirit';
- motivate staff;
- allow ideas to be explored;
- enable teams to plan;
- direct/assist in decision-making;
- identify the strengths of each team member and ensure they are utilised;
- offer support;
- provide positive feedback.

DEALING WITH CONFLICTS

A manager is expected to recognise when a conflict between two parties is brewing, and to intervene appropriately. Rarely is the wise course of action to let it develop naturally! The signs frequently manifest themselves in the form of destructive criticism, or by somebody refusing to take responsibility, expecting others to solve a problem, or parties breaking into sub-groups rather than wanting to discuss things as a whole or openly sharing the problem.

A manager must also be able to balance confidentiality with the need for knowledge. Conflicts are likely to be sensitive, and in some instances highly personal. Clearly you can respond appropriately only if you have sufficient knowledge of the position of both parties, but you may have to construct your advice on scanty information.

If a potential conflict could affect a child, then the manager should intervene and seek a resolution immediately. No other course of action is consistent with the nursery's primary responsibility being to children, under the provisions of the Children Act.

Strategies that a manager might employ in dealing with conflicts include:

- assertiveness coming from confidence in the culture of mutual respect;

- support and direction in the form of supervision for staff;
- recognition and feedback for the team member involved.

SELLING THE NURSERY

Maintaining occupancy of the nursery in accordance with budgets is fundamental to the ability to deliver the service in the manner intended. Chapter 6 looks at the financial reality of a nursery. However, it is important to appreciate at this point that, because fixed costs are so high, and because staff costs are such a high proportion of total costs, little can be cut out without radically affecting quality of service. If the nursery does not fill, costs are not covered. It is as simple as that.

As a manager you will know that the location of the nursery has been researched, and that there is a local market of parents who are likely to want to view the nursery. It is your job to ensure that each visiting parent gets an accurate picture of the service provided, and that they understand the terms on which a place can be reserved for their child.

In my experience, when there is a complaint about the service, it can be traced back to an initial misunderstanding of the service. In other words the parent's expectation differs from the explanation they heard when visiting at the outset.

The ability on the part of the manager to articulate fundamental principles and philosophies is thus critical. The manager will be expected to have a positive view on, for example, infants in nurseries and working parents. Secondly, those responsible for showing parents around the nursery must be clear about what service they are selling. It is not helpful, for instance, for a parent to believe they are buying a flexible service if they are required to bring and collect their child at the same time every day.

It will help if the features of the service – those aspects that you feel are important – can be 'translated' into benefits that parents can relate to. For example, the fact that the nursery may employ a comparatively higher ratio of staff to children may not mean anything to a parent. However, if you explain that staff are able to maximise their time with children as there are sufficient assistant staff members to prepare and clear activities, it begins to make sense. The difference between features and benefits is explained fully in Chapter 6.

When parents visit a nursery and appear to have found the service they are looking for – possibly after a long and anxious search – the last thing they wish to discuss is how to extricate themselves from the arrangement. However, the manager *must* be certain that the parents are wholly clear about the terms on which they are booking a place. Any nursery place is expensive, and if a place is being paid for but not used (such as during a notice period), few parents can let it go unnoticed. From the outset the parent must also understand that, although every endeavour will be made to balance the needs of parent and child, it is the nursery's duty to regard the child's needs as paramount.

Issues can arise here, typically over late collections and sick children policies, where parents are under pressure to maximise their working hours. At the same time, they are conscious that nursery policies cannot be compromised.

WORKING TO A PLAN

Chapter 6 is devoted to the construction and maintenance of a business plan. This can be a formal document, or drafted on the 'back of an envelope'. However, the benefits of having a frame-work to guide a manager's work are incalculable. Here we look at the importance in principle of working to a plan.

A manager must know what is expected in the job. There may be specific targets, such as an 85 per cent occupancy at all times, or a 50 per cent staff cost/turnover ratio. Or the targets may be looser, such as 'the manager is responsible for maximising occupancy'. But you need to know what they are. Targets also provide you with a framework for assessing your own performance, and there is no point in denying the inevitable trend towards performance-related pay schemes for managers. This is where an element of salary will be paid 'on commission' for achieving given financial results.

However, targets may not always be financial. They may include, for example, a requirement for the nursery to achieve Investor in People* status within the next 12 months (see Chapter 4), or that the nursery manual is expected to be revised and updated by the end of the year.

As a manager you are entitled to know against what criteria your performance will be assessed in order that you can decide how to prioritise your time and to accomplish tasks in the most efficient way. Such targets also provide you with a framework for reporting, and for assessment of your own accountability.

In more informal situations, working to a plan will mean a continuous dialogue with the nursery owner or management group, to ensure that you communicate over changes in plans and new priorities.

Working to a plan may also imply that training is required in order that you can build the appropriate skills. A classic example here is a manager who has no previous experience of bookkeeping to draw on, and is suddenly responsible for financial reporting in the nursery. A further common example is the daily use of a personal computer.

To achieve the objective of working to a plan, you will need to plan non-contact time carefully, for yourself and also for others who you will need to consult and liaise with, as part of fulfilling your reporting function.

Just as all staff are seriously hampered without a clear entitlement to non child-contact time, which they can devote to planning, observations, liaising with parents, etc., so too must the manager preserve and protect non nursery-contact time. This has resource implications but pays rich dividends in the attitude of others to the managerial role and its importance to the nursery.

FURTHERING THE QUALITY OF SERVICE

In the same way as planning appropriate activities for children relies on careful observation and record-keeping of development to date, so too developing the quality of the service as a whole requires a system to be in place for knowing how the nursery performs in terms of current quality criteria. There are a number of levels on which the nursery as a whole is expected to perform:

- against the nursery registration criteria set out by OFSTED;
- against the promises made to parents through the nursery contract and promotional literature, and what they have been told;
- against the standards expected within the policies of your employer
- against recognised contemporary thinking about children's entitlements, i.e. state-of-the-art early years practice.

There are many different perspectives on how to measure the quality of service offered and delivered. Probably the best known scheme is the Early Childhood Environment Rating Scale: Revised (ECERS-R) and Extension (ECERS-E)*, first developed at Morag House in 1991. The scale takes a developmental approach to quality, providing targets rather than absolute measurements. The scale has been criticised for not capturing the overall atmosphere of nursery settings, and the quality of interactions, particularly between adults and infants. In its analysis of the factors affecting quality, EPPE* used and then built on ECERS by conducting intensive case studies to explore practices within centres that had appeared on the scale to be achieving the best outcomes for children. EPPE* identified five key areas of practice that are particularly important:

- quality of adult/child verbal interactions;
- staff knowledge and understanding of the curriculum;
- knowledge of how young children learn;
- adult's skill in supporting children in resolving conflicts;
- helping parents to support children's learning at home.

Ann Mooney and Teresa Blackburn at the Thomas Coram Research Unit in London looked at the perspective of the child in *Children's Views on Childcare Quality* (DFES *Research Report RR482*)*, and identified these quality indicators:

- children's friendships are encouraged and supported;
- older children can 'hang out' with friends with minimum supervision;
- there is a range of activities which are regularly reviewed and changed or modified, to retain children's interest;
- activities and space is organised to accommodate the different needs and interests of both younger and older children;
- children and staff appear to have fun;
- children feel safe in the setting and there is a clear anti-bullying policy;
- staff facilitate activities/play and avoid interfering or telling older children what to do;
- staff avoid raising their voices when speaking to children;
- staff show respect for children, are caring, and take time to listen;
- in their interactions with children, staff take account of children's age, maturity and special needs;
- both male and female staff are employed;
- staff turnover is low to facilitate close relationships between children and adults;
- children have sufficient indoor and outdoor space;
- outdoor space is freely accessible for older children;
- the setting is comfortable with places to be quiet and relax;
- toilets are secure, clean and equipped appropriately;

- the setting offers places where children can be 'out of the eye' of adults;
- children have a choice of food that is attractive and enjoyable to eat, and ready access to a drink;
- children are encouraged to participate in decisions about the programme; their views are seen as important and there is evidence that they are taken seriously.

And finally, from the perspective of parents and what they seek when choosing childcare, The Ministry of Children and Youth Justice in Canada has surveyed and published on its website the following priorities that relate to quality for parents:

- relationship between caregivers and children;
- caregiver training and job satisfaction;
- physical setting;
- nature of programme;
- licensing (registration);
- attention to children allowed for in ratios/staffing;
- parent involvement.

Some years ago the DFES piloted a quality assurance scheme endorsement project (Investors in Children) to encourage all settings to continuously observe and evaluate their practice and, at the same time, reduce the proliferation of quality assurance schemes available to those that were sufficiently aspirational in terms of securing better outcomes for children. However, in the wake of the *Every Child Matters** agenda, and the development of the *Early Years Foundation Stage**, the department has withdrawn its investment in the scheme.

The question will continue to be whether quality is absolute, or a standard that is derived from the objectives of the setting itself. This debate aside, a manager should be in a position of knowing what aspects of service need attention and development.

Observation alone, however, will not improve the service and there needs to be a system in place for taking action on the observations made. My experience with our own nurseries has been that when this process was regarded as an 'audit' by central office staff, it was less effective than it has been more recently, when it became a quality 'observation'. The observation was undertaken by staff themselves and was a rotated responsibility. The monthly observation was discussed with a view to any issues being resolved by the staff team. Only if additional resources were needed, if a policy needed review or if special training was required was 'central office' involved. The staff team, led by the manager, owned and was held responsible for delivering the quality of service required. The standard of quality was implicit in the observation schedule and the system employed. This was a whole nursery performance system, as distinct from focusing on a particular member of the team or a particular aspect of practice. This is a holistic approach to quality assurance and drew out whether, from an overall perspective, the team and the company were offering what they promised. The approach also allowed all staff to appreciate what needed constant attention, and to deal with criticism in a positive way. An audit by 'head office' would have precluded most staff from this process. Such an approach fosters positive peer review.

PLANNING STAFF SHIFTS

A well-run nursery relies on everyone knowing the routine and the part they play in achieving it. Conversely, each and every member of staff must understand the implications and consequences for others of not cooperating and working with the routines as set out.

Given that most nurseries open for more hours each day than staff are required to work, there is likely to be a shift pattern, requiring a change of shifts for each individual on a weekly or monthly basis. Each member of staff needs to know the routine of each shift – the ebb and flow of each shift – and the differing tasks that need to be accomplished. Most importantly they need to know how one shift flows into another. This raises a number of important issues:

- the sense of responsibility that all staff must share in the whole nursery and for all children, while acknowledging particular strengths within the staff team;
- the need to engage children as often as possible throughout the day by having a rolling programming of activities on offer;
- the importance of targeting some activities for particular age or ability groups, as well as for mixed age or ability groups;
- compatibility of activities taking place alongside one another;
- planning in advance to alert staff to their responsibilities to consider how parents can be involved to prepare necessary resources, and to involve children in the planning process.

In any rota of activities there will be room for improvement, and although some 'deviations' can be planned for – holiday and sick absences, new children settling – you can never adequately allow for unexpected human 'failure'. Examples of the latter are expectations of new staff that are too high, personal ups and downs, lack of familiarisation time, children's moods, parents' demands.

Rota planning probably leans towards being an art rather than a science, and the target needs to be around making it work for most of the people, most of the time. We have learned that:

- Rotas must be given time and a chance to work, so stick with them for a sensible period.
- Provided that an appropriate range of activities is available to children, not every area of the nursery, nor every opportunity in the nursery, need always be available.
- All areas of the nursery in which planned activities are taking place must be supervised by staff allocated to that area.
- Care routines must never be compromised.
- Children can be engaged in planning, preparing for and tidying up activities.

The results of this practical approach to rota planning include the following:

- Quality of staff interaction with children is maintained.
- Staff gain fulfilment from the (fewer) activities they can properly engage in.
- Staff are less concerned with 'policing' and are able to release more time for children and parents.
- Children gain a positive attitude with regard to clutter and waste, and efficient space utilisation.

Planning human resources is dealt with in depth in Chapter 2.

COMMUNICATION

The principal ways we communicate are by the spoken word and in writing.

The spoken word

Good verbal communication is a two-way process. The speaker gives the listeners the opportunity to ask questions and make comments about what has been said in order to clarify.

The objective of verbal communication is to give a message in such a way as to be easily understood by the listeners – and to be sure that they understand it. There are, however, a number of barriers that get in the way, distorting or even shutting out the messages we try to send.

Barriers include physical distractions such as noise, temperature and lighting, and emotional distractions such as personal prejudices, experience, assumptions, or values and beliefs. Certain words can cause us to stop listening altogether. This can happen when people are moralising, threatening, criticising or just using jargon. So a good starting point in improving communication is to think about these barriers and prepare your communications with them in mind. Talk to people in an atmosphere free of interruptions and use words that don't rub people up the wrong way. While you can't do much about other people's emotions, you can do something about your own. Stay calm and neutral. If you sense emotional barriers in others, either keep your conversation brief and to the point, or postpone it.

Speaking effectively

It is generally believed that each of the following elements has a specific value in transmitting the 'true' message:

- words 7 per cent
- tone 35 per cent
- non-verbal or body language 58 per cent.

You may disagree with these percentages, but think about it for a moment. You have complete control over the words that you use. You have less control over the tone as your emotion begins to take over. Try saying the phrase 'Where did you go last night?' without emphasising any of the words. Repeat it, putting an emphasis on the first word, then again, this time emphasising the word 'you'. Three different 'true' messages will be conveyed to the listener and they will respond accordingly.

You have virtually no control over the non-verbal body language. Subconsciously your body will reveal what you really mean and think. If you sit with your arms and legs crossed, this is a defensive posture and indicates a hostile attitude towards the other person and/or the message. Sitting with your arms folded with your thumbs up shows a superior attitude. Leaning forward indicates interest or intimidation. People who rest their chin on one hand, and have a finger in or near their mouth, need reassurance. Those who rub their chin are thinking or making a decision and will not be listening to you, so stop talking. These are gestures, intentional movements, and should not be confused with body language. You may be able to control your body language at the beginning of a conversation, but the more you become involved, the more your subconscious will take over.

To back up the importance of body language at the beginning of a conversation, it should be noted that, of information relayed, 87 per cent is via the eyes, 9 per cent is via the ears, and 4 per cent is via the other senses (taste, touch, etc.).

A vital part of speaking effectively is being sure people understand what you mean. This is best done by asking a question. Never say 'Do you understand?' as this puts the onus on the listener and, rather than appear stupid, they will probably say 'yes'. If you say 'Have I explained that satisfactorily?' then the responsibility rests with you – the listener does not feel threatened and can answer honestly.

The following are the categories of questions that can be used depending upon the type of information you want in return:

- *Elaboration questions* – for information of a general nature:
  'Tell me about . . .'
  'Is there anything more?'
  'Would you elaborate on that please.'
- *Specification questions* – asking for more detailed information:
  'What precisely did she say?'
  'When was the last time this happened?'
- *Feeling questions* – when you want to know the emotional effect of something:
  'What did you feel when it happened?'
  'How do you feel when people are aggressive towards you?'
- *Opinion questions* – most people hold opinions about things and welcome the opportunity to express them:
  'What do you like about your present job?'
  'What do you least like about your job?'
  'What would you like that you don't have?'
- *Behavioural questions* – past behaviour is a good indicator of further behaviour:
  'How would you usually deal with a situation like this?'
  'What did you do the last time this happened?'
  'How did you react when . . .?'

Listening

Listening is a key part of speaking effectively. It is not enough just to concentrate and to understand; you need to let the other person know you have been listening.

The simplest way of indicating that you have listened to the speaker is by employing reflective techniques. Reflection is a form of summary of what has been said. It demonstrates empathy with the speaker.

Our responses fall into one of three types:

- apathy or dismissiveness – showing lack of interest in what has been said;
- sympathy – sharing the feeling of others, allowing their problem to become your problem;
- showing that you appreciate the other person's feelings or point of view without becoming involved or agreeing with them.

Imagine that someone says to you 'I am a bit down at the moment, my grandfather died yesterday. He was a lovely old chap and a real companion. I am going to miss him':

- apathetic response: 'Really, anyway, as I was saying . . .';
- sympathetic response: 'I know how you must feel, I felt dreadful for weeks after my aunt passed away last year';
- empathetic response: 'You must feel very upset'.

The written word

Many people feel uncomfortable with the written word. They put off writing reports and proposals and they dash off poorly conceived letters because they have not been taught to write in a way that is useful at work. The value of logically constructed, accurate, comprehensible and interesting written communication is considerable. If you realise that this is not one of your strengths, this section will hopefully help you feel more confident about putting pen to paper.

A whole new dimension to how we communicate has arrived with the advent of email. It is an unforgiving medium that does not allow for the benefits of face-to-face communication or even the lengthier, more complete way of writing a letter or paper. Email encourages us to distil what we want to say and sometimes to stray into 'texting' language. My solicitor tells me that you should never commit to email anything that you would not say in a signed letter, on letterhead. Email correspondence is valid in law and is, by its very nature, open to ambiguity and interpretation. If someone speaks to us in a monotone manner, it is difficult to really understand how they feel about what they are trying to communicate. How often have you misinterpreted a tone of voice, and how much more difficult is it to really appreciate the meaning of something completely toneless?

But we cannot, any longer, do without email, and one of its principal advantages is that it allows you to say something when you want to say it and reply when you want to reply, therefore letting you control when you communicate and avoid distractions from something else you want to get on with. Email has given us another choice in the way we communicate, alongside face-to-face meetings, telephone and letter writing. This can all begin to feel burdensome, and clearing emails, in particular, has become for some people, an extra task. An increasing number of people are choosing and making it known, how they like to communicate best – 'please contact me in the first instance by email, which I check twice a day' or 'please telephone/leave a message on my voicemail if this needs attention today' – to assist callers and make sure priorities are attended to appropriately.

However email does require us to write rather than speak. The general rules about writing are the same, regardless of the type of document you are producing, so it may be helpful to look at those rules first and follow up with a discussion of the different forms the writing may take. Written communications should be clear, readable, relevant and informative. The appendix to Chapter 3 provides some detailed guidelines for writing correctly.

PERSONAL WELL-BEING

'Stress management' is a common phrase today, but I prefer to think of it in terms of 'personal effectiveness' or 'handling pressure'. The word 'stress' has mainly negative connotations but actually there are many positive aspects to it. Sports people and actors rely on the increased flow of adrenalin to bring out their best performances. Nursery managers chairing important staff or parent meetings also experience feelings of excitement, nervousness and heightened awareness before and during their performance. They also feel drained and exhausted afterwards. This is all quite normal and should not cause concern. In itself, stress is not harmful, but it is best to avoid unnecessary pressures, to know how to cope with them if they do arise and to recognise the symptoms of too much stress.

Pressures of time

Many people worry about the fact that there are not enough hours in a day, and it may seem worse if you are, effectively, a one-person business having to do everything yourself.

It is possible to introduce some routine into your work without losing the flexibility that the nursery needs. If done thoughtfully, this will enable you to optimise the time spent doing what you really want to do, rather than worrying about administrative or operational details. You will also still have energy left for the other things you value in your life.

In any occupation there are tasks that must be done, those that should be done if possible, and those that would be satisfying or fun to do but which are not essential to the progress and success of the nursery. If you make a list of jobs to do at the beginning of each week or at the start of a day, this is one of several ways of categorising what, when and how you should tackle your work.

From the tasks that *must* be done, identify those that have to be done quickly and those that need some time and thought spent on them. Check that 'urgent' tasks really do have to be done – I am always intrigued by how many so-called urgent matters do not really need to be attended to until tomorrow and how many actually become obsolete. If anyone tells me that a task is urgent, I try to establish with them an actual time for completion so that I know what the deadline is.

When you have decided which jobs are important and which are urgent, you then allocate the necessary time to them. A good diary or daily planning sheet is useful in helping you give priorities to the demands on your time. It is also worth thinking about the time of day when you work best (i.e. morning or afternoon). When do you think most clearly, find it easiest to make decisions, and produce good written work?

When you have decided which is your best time, try to arrange your work programme around that and leave the routine, less important, matters to your least effective part of the day. Some of my colleagues who find it very difficult to wake up in the morning appreciate not having to rush into work early. Your timetable is more flexible when you have control over your day.

One way of reducing the feeling that you have to be working at full speed all day long is to pace yourself and vary the types of task you work on. Do not rush at everything indiscriminately – pause, put matters into perspective and introduce a change of pace into your work pattern. For example, intersperse the 'easy' piece of work with a few routine tasks such as the filing, making some phone calls, or treating yourself to a cup of coffee when you have finished a particularly difficult task. It is difficult to handle freedom and flexibility, if you have been used to a strict regime as a team member up until now.

Staying healthy

As I write this, the news tells me that BA is being accused of pressurising its staff to work when they have a minor illness, which leads to a longer period of feeling unwell. In a nursery setting, minor illnesses are extremely difficult to manage, given the risk of passing them on to colleagues, as well as to children. Clearly, working with generous ratios and a good back-up staffing plan can finesse such potentially sensitive situations, but many nurseries cannot afford this tolerance. The only real response is to put in place a culture and policies to promote well-being: relaxation, massage, yoga and exercise are all well-known methods, and some nursery groups are able to offer gym memberships to staff, and have reaped the benefits. Interestingly, nurseries where staff are required to eat with the children, i.e. where they are able to sit down and share proper and nutritious meals throughout the day rather than snacking in the staff room or 'on the go', report that their absenteeism levels are lower.

There are many pressures on nursery managers to succumb to an unhealthy life style. Invitations to seminars and meetings, tight deadlines, worrying about cash flow and future bookings, and feelings of isolation and helplessness all contribute to stress. You have to recognise where and when stress occurs. Try to identify and write down occasions, people and times that regularly increase your tension. Is it money, deadlines, lack of time, particular people? Just the act of knowing where the problems are helps you to find a solution, an alternative way of doing things.

When you really are under an unreasonable amount of stress, the physical symptoms should alert you to the situation. You may feel tense, have constant headaches or sore throats, suffer from digestive problems, keep going hot and cold, notice that your hands are trembling, and generally feel not well. You may also feel different. You may be aware that you feel panicky, always on the defensive and generally depressed. Your behaviour will change – perhaps you are becoming aggressive, relying on drink, cigarettes or drugs to calm you down, and you may become accident prone.

All of these signs mean that you have to stand back and take stock of the situation, and take the necessary steps towards a healthier way of living. Except in extreme medical cases, you may be able to heal yourself with some simple resolutions.

Eat sensibly, exercise properly and rest well

It is tempting to keep on working if you are busy and not have breaks for lunch or a mid-morning cup of coffee. Part of pacing yourself properly is to know when to take breaks to rest your brain, to move your limbs and have a change of surroundings. Taking lunch does not place you under an obligation to stop for a full hour.

Some kind of exercise is beneficial to everyone. This does not mean rushing to the squash court once every six months to prove that you are still young and active. Exercise should be regular, within your capabilities, and you should always warm up and 'warm down' before and after any physical activity. Much serious illness in busy people is due to irregular strenuous exercise without preparing the body adequately for the unaccustomed exertion.

The body needs rest as well as exercise if the correct balance is to be maintained. Some people need more sleep than others but, however long you need, make sure that you have enough. There will always be times when circumstances mean you have to work extremely hard for a few days, and this may result in only a few hours' sleep each night during that period. The body can easily cope with this if you are fit, but will react badly if it becomes a regular occurrence.

Have regular check-ups

This is particularly important as you get older or if you have a history of illness. If you object in principle to belonging to one of the private health schemes, your doctor will be pleased to give you a general examination to test that everything is well.

In addition to modern medicine, you may wish to consult practitioners of complementary or alternative medicine. For example, if you suffer from back pain, you are as likely to find relief from a chiropractor as from a doctor. The nature of nursery work places heavy stresses on the body – for instance, lifting heavy toddlers on to a changing mat many times in a day, or bending to pick up babies. You might consider learning the Alexander Technique, which teaches you to 'fine tune' your body, how to bring it back into balance. To what extent you use these complementary methods will depend on your own beliefs.

There is also much you can introduce into the nursery to relieve such physical stress on staff, such as adult-height chairs for sitting in to receive babies from parents, and steps to enable toddlers to reach the changing surface themselves.

Learn to relax

Take regular bouts of proper relaxation and build them into your day. This is a time for deep unwinding, not just five minutes sitting at your desk with a cup of tea. You can learn how to meditate or devote time to a personal way of relaxing such as walking, music or sport. The time set aside for this must be preserved – and must not be the first thing to be sacrificed as soon as work builds up.

The office

For people who have not been used to running an office or doing all the administrative work themselves, the new routines and details may prove a source of stress. For an office to provide a sound support for you and your work, it is worth spending time setting up the systems that will actually help you and not just create frustration.

If you really hate office work but cannot afford any help yet, arrange a routine so that you do the filing, type up the invoices, update the accounts and check the stationery supplies regularly and efficiently. In that way you will spend as little time as is necessary on these tasks. They have to be done, and you can get yourself into all sorts of trouble, operational and legal, if they are neglected. If you are in a situation that makes it extremely difficult to get office work done – for example in a small nursery the manager may be included in the ratio of staff to children – you could investigate the possibility of having a business administration student from the local college come in to help one day a week. This provides them with a useful placement, and you with an identified time for routine office work to be dealt with.

I would emphasise the importance of the design of your workplace, particularly in relation to the way it affects you physically. An office should be well ventilated but not too cold. Also, if you have computers and photocopiers in a smallish space, do not allow them to overheat.

Many people who operate computer keyboards have not learned to type on a traditional typewriter. While this does not affect their ability to operate the machine, it may mean that they do not know how to sit properly, or understand where their hands and arms should be in relation to the keyboard. There are increasing numbers of cases of repetitive strain injury (RSI) being reported among people who use keyboards often. This is a very painful inflammation of the joints, usually the wrists, elbows and up to the shoulders and neck in serious cases. It occurs through repeating particular actions over a long period of time, and when it first appears many patients and doctors think it is rheumatism. For anyone who uses a keyboard, the advice is to make sure you take regular breaks, not only from straining your eyes looking at the screen, but also from repeating the action of striking the keys. Stop every twenty minutes or so and do something else for a short while. In extreme cases, sufferers may not regain the full use of their hands if they do not heed the first warning pains.

Another common factor in RSI cases is that keyboards are often too high in front of the operator. Ideally your shoulders should be down and your hands and elbows in a straight line, parallel to the floor and level with the keyboard. This means buying a good chair.

Be fit for life – maintaining the balance

One way to minimise the negative aspects of stress is to strike the right personal balance between work, home and leisure. This balance will be different for every individual and may change during the various phases of your life, so it is worth reviewing your priorities from time to time.

During your first two or three years as a manager you will probably be tempted to become totally immersed in your work. It is at this time that even the most understanding partners and friends will find that their patience is sorely tested. Most people will recognise your need to build up the nursery, but your true friends will also persuade you to honour your holiday commitments, join the local gym or take up photography – or anything that will keep your work in perspective. Most importantly, discuss what is happening with the people with whom you are most deeply involved. They will also be picking up the phone when your staff ring on a Sunday night to say they are sick.

MANAGING YOURSELF AND OTHERS

Analysing your objectives will lead to a priority order of tasks. The next step is to look at *your own* strengths and weaknesses in relation to these tasks. Remember, you are doing two things: starting up or maintaining a childcare project, and secondly, securing its permanence and stability by treating it as a *business.*

There are three areas in which leadership and management need to be apparent:

- technical authority;
- managing people;
- managing the business.

How would you rate your abilities against the following list, taken from the National Westminster Bank's *Guide to the Preparation of a Business Plan?*

I am self-disciplined and do not let things drift.
I have the full support of my family.
I am ready to put in 7 days a week, if necessary.
I can get on well with people.
I can make careful decisions.
I can cope under stress.
I do not give up when the going gets tough.
I can learn from mistakes.
I can take advice.
I am patient, and I expect a long haul.
I can motivate people.
I am in good health.
I am enthusiastic.
I know about the risks.
I have specific aims.

In order to plan what additional *human* resources you need, you must first decide what you are going to do as a manager, and the role you will play in relation to others. You will be making a broad transition of attitudes from acting on instructions to directing and supervising the carrying out of instructions you have given. You will be in a position of authority, requiring assertiveness and evaluation skills, rather than compliance and response. Although you will retain accountability for the actions of others, you will not be *doing* everything. You will start to rely on others to come up with ideas, and then assess them and make decisions. And you will become a listener and supporter of others. This last quality is often the most difficult for a new manager to learn. Nursery managers are exceptional in this role, it being a central part of the training and experience as a nursery nurse.

Managing yourself

It is hard to see how anyone can seriously expect to become an effective business manager until they can first manage their own activities.

There are three aspects to managing yourself that need to be kept under regular review and have a major impact on the ability of the rest of your staff to be able to perform. The first is managing your own time – vital if you are to win back the opportunity to think and plan; the second is managing meetings, or other people's time – vital if your team is going to have to change to do their job effectively; the third is effective communication.

Managing time

Most owner-managers have a false impression of how they use their time and how it affects their performance. There is a strong body of research that suggests that a typical MD could improve his or her output by at least 105 per cent and save time by as much as 20–30 hours in a typical working week. A prize such as having an 8- or 9-day fortnight at your disposal is surely worth a modest investment of time and energy. There are many time management systems on the market, but you can realise many of the benefits yourself immediately without any expense.

Step 1

Have a daily and weekly 'to do' list. Most senior people in business have a diary scheduling meetings and the like but do not have lists of key tasks to be completed each day and each week. It follows that, without a set of daily objectives, key priorities cannot be established, nor can you commit to driving hard to achieve those objectives.

Step 2

Establish the key priorities. A manager's day is made up of different types of priorities:

- 'A' priorities are highly essential activities that must be completed or progressed substantially.
- 'B' priorities are less essential activities that can be deferred because the time element is less critical and the impact on job performance is lower.
- 'C' priorities are non-essential activities that can be scrapped, screened out, handled by other people or handled at low-priority times.
- 'X' priorities are activities that require immediate attention. There may be queries, requests for information, crises and emergencies, boss demands or interruptions. You can have 'AX', 'BX' or 'CX' priorities.

One of the golden rules of time management is based on the Pareto or 80/20 rule. This suggests that 80 per cent of your performance will come from 20 per cent of your activities, and 20 per cent of your performance will come from 80 per cent of your activities.

When you assess your own time usage and your own performance in the day, you will find that the majority of your time has been spent on lower priority work. Log the following:

- For each activity calculate the time you spent on it.
- For each activity assign an ABCX priority.
- Work out the total time spent on ABCX priorities as a percentage of the total day.
- Ask a very frank question about your 'A' priority activities. 'Did I achieve what I intended to achieve?'
- Estimate the time you could have saved, by better discipline and control, on each low-priority activity.
- Make a judgement about your achievement on the day: how much 'continuous' time you spent on your top-priority work and how much 'total' time you could have devoted to high-priority work if you had exercised better control and discipline.

When you go through this assessment you may find that you are not spending enough time on your top-priority work in order to achieve, and that the majority of time (which could be as high as 60 per cent or 70 per cent) will be spent on low-priority work of which you could have saved at least 20 per cent by better control and discipline.

Review how you spend your time

This is a simple technique whereby you sum the total amount of time (in percentages) you spend in certain categories of activities. Typical C categories are: meetings, telephone, correspondence, project work, report writing, reading, etc. Each manager will have different categories and different times, but managers usually find they spend at least 40–50 per cent of a typical day in some sort of meeting.

If you made an assessment of the amount of time you could save by 'crisper' management of these activities, you would find that your time saving could be between 20 per cent and 30 per cent. The three priority areas for time saving and better self-management are delegation, meetings, and personal organisation.

Keeping a log

You can make a start on improving your time management by keeping a daily log for three or four days, reviewing how you spent your time – and look for ways to save time, improve performance or delegate tasks.

Managing meetings

Meetings consume between one and three days of a business week. It follows that anything that can be done to make them more effective must be good news. Meetings are vital. They are a forum for exchanging ideas and gaining fresh thinking, a way to communicate complex information, a way to gain consensus and commitment to key decisions. Unfortunately, most people see most meetings as a complete waste of time – including the person who called the meeting! The following are some points to help make your meetings more effective.

Define the purpose

Know exactly what you expect to achieve. Meetings without set objectives demotivate people. The purpose might be to inform staff of new initiatives/procedures (in many instances a memo would be a quicker, cheaper and just as efficient a way of doing this); it might be to identify and resolve a particular problem, to review progress and give people an opportunity to express their views. Asking yourself what would happen if the meeting was not held is a great help in defining its objectives.

Decide who should attend

The fewer participants the better if the meeting is going to achieve its objectives in a reasonable length of time. However, research has shown that larger groups often come up with sounder decisions than individuals or a small number of people – but take much longer to do so.

Ensure everyone prepares properly

A meeting is much less stressful if all the participants have prepared in advance, yourself included. If possible, circulate beforehand a note giving notice of the meeting with the agenda items. The note should state the purposes of the meeting and probable duration (to give people a chance to organise the rest of their day).

An agenda is vital for any meeting. It acts as the control device, establishing order and sequence, assigning tasks and providing guidelines for the timing of each item. If a meeting is called on the spur of the moment, it should still have an agenda, even if it is just jotted down on the back of an envelope. An agenda sent in advance gives people a chance to do their homework.

If participants need to have absorbed specific information before they can discuss an item, it is much better to send this out well in advance since nothing wastes more time than people sitting reading during a meeting.

Be a good listener

People who chair meetings need to listen more carefully than anyone else in the group since it is their job to make sure the real point of someone's contribution isn't being missed. They need to pick the right moment to move on, clarify points when people are getting in a muddle, and summarise all the views when it is time to push for a decision.

Involve all the participants

People are likely to feel far more committed to the meeting and decisions reached if they have had a chance to say their piece. And, indeed, people should not be at the meeting unless they have something to contribute. It is the leader's task to ensure that everyone has a chance to participate.

Use open-ended questions to get people to talk (questions that start with words such as how, what, why, when – these are impossible to answer with a Yes or No).

Make positive noises throughout the session ('Anybody add to that?' 'Any more?') to encourage the shy. Check round the group ('Let's see where we all stand on that; Terri, you first') – this not only forces people to speak but also generally motivates the meeting.

Closed questions (those that begin with do, can, are, which – these are usually answerable with a Yes or a No) can be used to bring the talkative to a halt.

Keep the meeting on course

Red herrings and ramblings are the chief dangers when you are trying to stay on course and keep to time limits. There are polite ways to stem the speaker's flow: cough, lean forward, raise your eyebrows, or use the more positive 'We're getting off the point aren't we?' Don't be too tolerant with people who regularly take the meeting off at a tangent or you'll lose the respect of the others who want to see your hand firmly on the wheel.

Control aggression

Conflict can be healthy in that it encourages new ideas and new ways of solving problems. It is the chairperson's job to ensure that everyone has a fair say and a fair hearing even if they are disagreeing. However, some control may need to be exercised if things are getting particularly ugly or someone with strong views is being very vocal.

You must avoid taking sides or apportioning blame – this always provokes an argument, and the chairperson who loses his or her temper loses credibility in the process.

Check that everyone understands

You need to know both that the rest of the group is not at cross-purposes with the speaker, and that they understand what he or she is trying to convey. So check assumptions by asking following questions: 'So you mean that if we improve X we'll get better results from Y?' Make a habit of providing a verbal summary of what has been said.

Decide on action

The purpose of meetings is not to impose decisions but to reach decisions by consensus. Once decisions have been made, remind everyone of what they are, define clearly how they are to be acted upon, by whom and by when.

Memories being short, it is essential to produce minutes (or at least some notes) of every meeting, if for no other reason than to prevent subsequent arguments over who was responsible for what. Another of the chairperson's tasks is to ensure that this is done, although he or she may well prefer to delegate minute-taking to someone else in the group.

The minutes should be brief and strictly factual, describing what happened without distortion or comment, sticking to suggestions and proposals with the names of the people who made them, actions agreed and the name of the person responsible for each action.

Minutes of a meeting should be sent out within a couple of days, especially if there are a number of actions to be carried out. If it is not possible to do this, then a summary may be made of the actions agreed and copies distributed immediately after the meeting. A sheet similar to the one shown in Figure 3.4 may be used as a simple way of recording actions during a meeting.

MEETING				Date:
Action Ref:	Action	By whom	By when	Date completed
Chairperson's signature:				

FIGURE 3.4 Summary of actions

Make sure decisions are implemented

If the meeting was worth having, the decisions are worth implementing, so your job doesn't stop when the meeting finishes. You need to monitor progress, which may involve holding a follow-up meeting, asking for interim reports or carrying out day-to-day checks.

UNDERSTANDING BEHAVIOURS

There are three interrelated sets of needs that a nursery manager will have to satisfy: task needs, team needs, and individual needs.

Task needs

The difference between a team and a random crowd is that the team has some common purpose or goal. Without this common objective, it would not stick together as a group. If a team does not achieve the required result or output, it will become frustrated.

TASK-ORIENTED BEHAVIOUR

- Agree objective
- Plan and allocate resources
- Make decisions
- Control progress
- Review and evaluate

Organisations have a task to provide a service, to cover costs, or even just to survive. So anyone who manages others has to achieve results.

Team needs

The group must be held together. People need to work in a coordinated fashion in the same direction. Teamwork will ensure that the team contribution is greater than the sums of its parts. Conflict within the team must be used effectively: argument can lead to new ideas, or to tension and lack of cooperation.

TEAM-ORIENTED BEHAVIOUR

- Select the right people
- Communicate with them
- Encourage
- Harmonise
- Use humour
- Coordinate

Individual needs

Within working groups, individuals also have their own set of motivational needs: the need to know what their responsibilities are, how they will be judged, how well they are doing. They need an opportunity to show their potential, take on responsibilities and receive recognition for good work.

INDIVIDUAL-ORIENTED BEHAVIOUR

- Trust and respect
- Listen
- Identify training needs
- Appraise
- Delegate
- Develop
- Motivate
- Recognise and praise

The manager's job must be to satisfy all three areas of need by achieving the task, building the team and satisfying individual needs. If managers concentrate only on tasks, for example in going all out for achieving output while neglecting the training and motivations of their people, they may do very well in the short term. Eventually, however, those people will give less than they know they are capable of. Similarly, neglecting the task will not get the maximum contribution from employees. They will lack the real sense of achievement that comes from accomplishing the task.

Nurseries need to give some attention to their internal communication. Staff tend to be in highly motivated small teams, spending a lot of time together at work and socially. As the nursery grows in numbers, sheer size will start to crack the foundations of this group, and the introduction of new people without the original motivation will change the flavour of relationships. It is at this point that the manager will consciously have to introduce ways and means of getting the team together and keep them facing the right way. Involving your team in the preparation of a business plan can, in itself, be a good way of providing coordination to a growing business.

It is amazing how many business people expect a team to work without any practice. After all, it presumably doesn't work this way for a football team. The way to build up a team is to find many formal and informal ways of bringing them together: cascade briefing, social events, special project teams, happy hours. Fun is actually quite compatible with profit. The importance of informal contact between people, as a way of building productive networks, cannot be over emphasised, but again it won't take place without the mechanism to make it happen. A high-performing team relies on the nurture of a strong culture that continuously reminds staff that they work in an organisation that has:

- an atmosphere of trust, empowerment and meritocracy;
- a strong vision, strong values and measurable practices;
- aligned its values and branding with those of parents, clients and other stakeholders;
- a programme for staff to be influenced by the practice of others.

APPENDIX TO CHAPTER 3

Language

The written word in business should be simple and straightforward. Many people think that reports and letters have to be written in a different language from the spoken word, but this usually leads to complex sentences and the misuse of words. If you have any problems writing a sentence or paragraph, try saying it aloud. This usually helps to clarify your thoughts.

Although you should always be aware of the person who will be reading what you write, and so use the appropriate words and way of presenting the material, you do not have to use a different kind of English for each type of reader. Your aim is clarity. You are not trying to bewilder or mystify the reader or make life difficult for yourself.

- *Be clear.* Do not allow room for ambiguity or wrong assumptions. For example the following sentence could have two meanings: 'The mother told the member of staff she had made a mistake.' Who made the mistake?
- *Keep it short and simple.* As a writer you are aiming at clarity of expression, balance of ideas and arguments, and interest in what has been written. You should therefore keep sentences and paragraphs short and simple.

  It is advisable to break long sentences down into shorter ones to avoid overusing punctuation. As a sentence grows in length, the rate of reading and comprehension slows down.

  Do not use many words when a few will do, or complicated phrases to express a simple idea. For example, 'in the event that we are in a position to undertake' can be expressed as, 'if we can', and 'endeavour to ascertain' can be expressed as 'try to find out'.

  It is generally easier to read statements that use the active voice rather the passive voice. For example, 'It was declared by John' is better as 'John said', and 'The undersigned was not telephoned by your assistant' can be 'Your assistant did not phone me'.
- *Keep jargon in its place.* You may be able to use technical words for some readers but you may have to explain them to others. Do not resort to jargon unless it is appropriate to the audience. Generally, your technical words and phrases will be incomprehensible to anyone apart from your staff (e.g. 'Christian's gross motor skills are underdeveloped').
- *Avoid clichés.* For example: 'At this moment in time the general standard of English leaves much to be desired, but it goes without saying that at the end of the day it will all come out in the wash!'
- *Use punctuation to help the reader.* Punctuation does for writing what pauses do for speech. It is often better to break long sentences down into shorter ones than to worry about whether to use brackets or dashes. The importance of punctuation is shown in the following examples, which use the same words but mean completely different things:

  'Teenagers, who drive carelessly, should not be allowed to have a driving licence.'

  'Teenagers who drive carelessly should not be allowed to have a driving licence.'

The correct use of English

Unfortunately many people have not had the benefit of learning the rules of written English, even though we pay attention to such disciplines when we learn a foreign language. Consequently, by the time they come to study and work, they do not feel at ease with the demands of producing the wide range of written documents required of them. This section looks at some of the pitfalls.

Spelling

There are those who can and those who can't. If you have a spelling checker on your computer, make sure that it is appropriate for your work. That is, does it have English or American spelling – e.g. programme or program; centre or center?

Couples

Some words look and sound similar but cause confusion. Examples of such 'couples' include:

- principle/principal
- practise/practice
- stationery/stationary
- dependent/dependant
- complement/compliment.

Do you know the difference between them in all cases?

Similar words

There are other pairs of words that are similar in sound or spelling but that have distinct meanings. They include:

- practical/practicable
- disinterested/uninterested
- continual/continuous
- effect/affect.

Are you sure when these should be used?

Apostrophes

Apostrophes are used in two ways. The first use is to indicate that letters or figures have been omitted (e.g. It's for It is; or '95 for 1995). The second use is to indicate what is known as the 'possessive case' – that

97

something belongs to a word or person (e.g. the book's pages = pages belonging to the book; or the child's toys = toys belonging to the child). Apostrophes should *not* be used to indicate plural as in 'hot drink's served here' or 'hundred's of jobs for temp's'.

- 'It's' means 'It is'. The apostrophe shows that something has been left out – in this case, the 'i' of 'is'. In 'What's your name?' it is the 'i' of 'What is your name?' that the apostrophe replaces.
- 'We have dealt with our parent's problems for many years.' Parent's = the problems of our (one) parent. Parents' = the problems of our (several) parents.

There is nothing to hide in finding writing difficult. It probably was not given the attention it deserved in college. Be honest with yourself and spend some time confronting the problem and practising the skill. You will be a more confident manager as a result.

Letter writing

As a manager you will have to write letters, and for most people this takes practice. Even if you do not have a natural flair for the written word, follow a few simple rules and your letters will be clear and present a good image of you and the work you do.

Prepare thoroughly

- Make sure that you are addressing the recipient of the letter in the correct way, or the way she/he prefers.
- Collect together the necessary support material, such as previous correspondence and relevant files, so you have to hand all the facts you need.
- Note down what you need to say in a logical order. At first you may have to write down most of the letter, but as you become more confident you will manage with a list of headings to remind you of what you want to say.
- Research the extra information you need such as unusual spellings of names, places or products, references, enclosures and extra copies. Also consider how you will address the recipient. Is he 'Dear Sir', 'Dear Mr Jackson', 'Dear David' or 'My Dear Dave'? The salutation may set the tone for the rest of the letter.

You are now ready to write the letter.

Chapter 4

Investing in people

- Professional development
- Leader-generated development
- The Investor in People* scheme
- A career development model
- Delegating
- Recruiting staff
- Appendix

PROFESSIONAL DEVELOPMENT

> The final suggestion, the final statement, has to be not a deliberate statement but a helpless one. It has to be what you can't avoid saying, not what you set out to say.
>
> Jasper Johns

Ongoing learning should have as much to do with the 'why' of what we do as the 'how'. This is, in essence, the difference between a professional development approach and one of training for skills. Better and better outcomes for children will only be reached through purposeful reflection and challenging ourselves to take another step forward, sometimes to take a risk, but always to seek inspiration from others and be open to new ideas. Moving beyond the daily activity of delivering good early years practice is hard: you seem to be satisfying regulators, parents and your employer, so why go further? We have discussed in earlier chapters the child development, and personal development reasons for this; however, a further reason is to think about how your nursery will stand out from the crowd – how your service will be recognised as being 'cutting edge'. In this podcast age we all have access to the same knowledge and information; what matters is the inspiration we draw from it to feed our passions and influence what we do. Our creativity is what makes the difference now. What can we make of this new idea, what potential does it have to improve outcomes for children and families, how can we best share it amongst our team? A manager/leader can help to prompt such curiosity and conversation by offering time and place for them to happen and by providing some starting points.

You could begin with a challenging quote from a recognised thought-leader, for instance, using a quote from the poet Edna St Vincent Millay for inspiration:

> The world is mine: blue hill, still silver lake, broad field, bright flower, and the long white road. A gateless garden and an open path; my feet to follow, and my heart to hold.
>
> St Vincent Millay, 2001*

What can this passage lead us to think about in relation to our practice? For me, it speaks of personalising things, giving purposeful attention to the details of what we do so that aspirations for each child can fly high.

 100

Another example comes from a child at a Reggio Emilia school:

I can tell how much I have grown by myself, because when I stand up I feel a lot taller – see where my head comes to!

Reggio Emilia*

This reminds me that children are able, the way they think is valid, and that our role in making visible children's desire to investigate is important.

Does the team agree with those interpretations? How can they be reflected in day-to-day practice? Have they helped to reconnect them with their passion for working with children? Can we demonstrate and evidence how those interpretations may be true? Who has a vignette that illustrates how the interpretation is demonstrated in daily work? Could we use the interpretation usefully in our marketing material? What needs further attention to make that interpretation visible to others?

Professional development is about getting staff to think deeply about what they do – experience plus reflection is the learning that lasts.

Ongoing learning is not the lonely province of the leader, the owner, the HR function or the Board: it is the immediate responsibility of those to whom it happens. HR may well act as a postroom for the organisation of training courses and the selection of appropriate developmental processes, but the learning itself is the province of individuals themselves, led by a *learning leader* – the nursery manager.

In order to retain good people for as long as possible, they need to be included, nurtured and developed and to keep learning with you. If this is done, you can honestly state that frequently abused term, 'people are our greatest asset'.

It is a current trend for managers to be held accountable as counsellors and coaches of their teams. Effective indications of success in this area are staff turnover, sickness levels and the rate at which staff develop.

The context for management and organisational development has changed. Thanks to the work of Charles Handy, John Constable and Roger McCormick, in the late 1980s, various issues have since led to the development of the *Management Charter Initiative** and the wealth of national competencies for all managers, through National Vocational Qualifications. For people in early years' services, management competencies will become apparent in NVQ level 4. There are currently a variety of early childhood studies courses, ranging from NVQ level 2 through to postgraduate degrees (see Chapter 3). At under-graduate level, courses do not usually provide an opportunity for in-depth study of the practical application of aspects of theory of early childhood development.

Postgraduate courses are more often workplace-based, thereby offering an environment for those wishing to bring knowledge, skills and experience to bear on a pertinent problem within their professional situation, and to observe the effects over a substantial period of time. Up until recently the best route forward has been to explore NVQ assessor competencies, which provide education and development. Higher qualifications introduced into the sector relatively recently, such as the Early Years Foundation Degree and the *National Professional Qualification in Integrated Centre Leadership**, incorporate much stronger management and leadership modules, although these are unlikely to be accessed by the majority of the workforce not aspiring to leadership positions. (See Figure 4.1.)

Another initiative, which is catching on fast, is the *Personal Development Agreement*. This is a contract between the individual and the organisation,

---

CODE OF CONDUCT

When your organisation joins the MCI, it makes a pledge to both current and future managers through the ten-point Code of Practice.

Chief Executives will communicate and demonstrate to all managers their commitment to this Code. It is a formal recognition of the importance of management education and development. Your organisation will promise:

1 To improve leadership and management skills throughout its structure.
2 To encourage managers continuously to develop their management and leadership skills.
3 To provide a coherent framework for self-development within the context of corporate goals.
4 To ensure that the development of managerial expertise is a continuous process, fully integrated with the work flow.
5 To provide ready access to relevant learning and development opportunities – both internal and external – with requisite support and time released, appropriate to the organisation.
6 To encourage and help managers acquire recognised relevant qualifications.
7 To participate actively in the appropriate MCI Networks.
8 Directly and through Networks, to strengthen links with management education sources, ensuring that the training offered will best complement management development programmes-matching corporate needs and future requirements.
9 To contribute to closer links with educational establishments.
10 To appoint a director or equivalent to oversee the fulfilment of these undertakings; to review progress annually and, after evaluating the contribution to performance, set new targets for both the individuals and the organisation; and to publicise highlights from the review and the new targets.

FIGURE 4.1 The Management Charter Initiative Code of Conduct

which states that, for a given output of work and the achievement of mutually agreed targets of performance and behaviour, the organisation will encourage activities of the individual to develop personally and, by extension, the organisation.

Note that it is a 'personal development' agreement, not a technical training one. It is about more than getting the job done, via the inclusion, competence and development route outlined in Chapter 1, and it has four aspects:

- personal development;
- professional development;
- team development;
- organisational development.

For each individual a time and money budget needs to be agreed. These details can be incorporated in a regular appraisal system. This facilitates a linking between personal needs and organisational targets. The personal development aspect can cover anything from physical fitness to studying for a part-time degree, the essence being personal challenge and growth.

This will be least influenced by organisational targets, and consequently is the most overlooked in terms of an activity that is seen as fruitful and worthwhile, altogether too soft for many managers. However, just as we believe, in our approach to children's learning, that care and education are inextricably linked, so we should be well placed to pursue achievement through nurturing, rather than accepting the more macho approach of bringing things under one's control and imposing one's will.

There is another reason why, once we realise it, we are in a good position to follow the people development path. Parents rate highly the continuity of nursery staff. It must therefore make commercial sense to bring on our own people, in whom we have *already made* the investment. If we do not, it diminishes the perceived worth of existing staff and de-energises them.

LEADER-GENERATED DEVELOPMENT

This involves setting mutually agreed targets with individuals and teams, planning how to achieve them and delegating the authority to get on with it, and then monitoring the reality – the 'eyes on, hands off' approach. This can be as simple as the 'One Minute Manager' notion of one minute's praise, one minute's criticism, per person, per day.

The basis of this approach lies in understanding that coaching is not teaching. It is not telling people what and how to do something, but getting them to develop a closer and closer focus on the way they do it – to question, monitor and give feedback.

A more nurturing and empathetic approach is to become available as a counsellor, putting oneself in the other's position and to start from where they are, rather than question the way they have gone about tackling the problem to date.

'Mentoring' is a further means of developing staff, more popular in the USA than here. Someone more senior is given responsibility to bring the individual on and to make best use of their contribution. The mentor is not the nursery manager or line manager and is generally concerned with wider issues than just performance in the job. There can, however, be problems when mentoring is formally established. Mentors can become patronising, or have their own motivations for being a mentor – perhaps wishing to muster support for a particular work method.

'Job rotation' is frequently overlooked as a low-cost means of extending the experience of staff and providing new challenges for those seeking promotion. It fits in with the concept of self-development, and complements inclusion and shared culture as fundamental aspects of investing in people.

The more traditional development and external training courses, although more expensive, can add a wholly different dimension to individual and organisational learning. Participants in open courses (i.e. those with no entry qualification required) rate their usefulness as:

- getting views and experiences of others in similar positions;
- getting views and experiences of those outside the industry;
- making contacts for future career possibilities;
- having a break from usual routine;
- gathering new knowledge, skills and techniques.

So, they generate different perspectives, encourage debate and broaden understanding. It is, however, questionable whether they contribute to performance and behaviour – the essence of competence.

Tailor-made, in-company courses, on the other hand, are gaining in favour. They can focus on key groups, on specific topics and be highly practical – allowing participants to return to their job and put something they have learned into practice immediately. At worst, as the facilitator or speaker will have been briefed by the organisation itself, they can reinforce existing prejudices and block change.

THE INVESTOR IN PEOPLE* SCHEME

*Every Child Matters** sets out the common core of skills and knowledge expected of everyone who works with children. They are described under six broad headings:

- effective communication and engagement with children;
- child development;
- safeguarding and promoting the welfare of the child;
- supporting transitions;
- multi-agency working;
- sharing information.

Acquisition of these skills and this knowledge will fulfil expectations of nursery staff related to children; however, as we have noted earlier, there are now likely to be other stakeholders. Parents will expect the organisation that owns/runs the nursery to be competent, and parents, as well as the organisation as the employer, will expect the leader/manager to achieve goals that will go beyond the achievement of successful outcomes for children. This is where Investors in People, both as a discipline and as recognition for strong management, can help.

The Investors in People scheme is a national scheme that encourages organisations to recognise the importance of developing staff to meet business objectives. The scheme recognises that every organisation is unique, just as every employee is an individual. But, in the same way, there are certain factors that are common to all. Organisations employ people and, whatever the business, the way those people perform will be a major factor in its success or failure.

People who are flexible and adaptable, willing to learn and enthusiastic about the business and about their work must be valuable assets in any organisation. Investor in People* is based on the experiences of all types and sizes of successful UK companies that have proved that performance is improved by a planned approach to:

Setting and communicating business goals
Developing people to meet these goals
so that
What people can do and are motivated to do
Matches what the business needs them to do

105

Working towards meeting the Investor in People* standard will in itself bring many benefits along the way, through the increased involvement and contribution of people at all levels within the organisation.

Being recognised as an Investor in People* will increasingly be found to be of value, in the eyes of potential recruits as well as current employees, those with a stake in the business, and ultimately parents and suppliers.

An Investor in People* improves individuals' performances by planning and taking action to improve the skills, knowledge. motivation, commitment, confidence and job satisfaction of all its people. Actions include developmental activities like:

- induction of new recruits;
- communications with employees;
- agreeing targets and standards for competence;
- encouraging attainment of appropriate qualifications and career progression;
- management development.

An Investor in People* also takes action to ensure that all employees are aware of the contribution they can make to success – and that people then have the opportunity to make that contribution.

The national standard is a benchmark against which all organisations can measure their own commitment to and effectiveness in investing in people. The standard is founded on the four principles of commitment, planning, action and evaluation:

- *Commit* to investing in people to achieve business goals.
- *Plan* how skill needs of individuals and teams are to be developed to achieve these goals.
- *Act* to develop and use necessary skills in a well-defined and continuing programme.
- *Evaluate* progress towards goals, value achieved and future needs.

Clearly it is possible to realise some benefits without going through the full Investor in People* process, but the four principles of the standard interrelate. Working through them step by step will provide a focus and structure for your efforts. Once an organisation has been assessed as meeting the standard, it is publicly recognised as an Investor in People*.

Many of the companies that have achieved the standard or who are working towards it are small or medium-sized businesses. In fact the process is more straightforward for smaller organisations with face-to-face communications and few tiers of management.

Becoming an Investor in People* will need commitment and an investment of time, from you downwards. But it is not necessarily about doing more training or spending more money. It is about doing the training that is essential for the nursery and developing people more effectively to achieve your goals.

The actual cost will depend on what you do already, the resources you have, how you match up to the national standard, and what you have to do to meet it. Your first priority will be to take charge of progress – or make someone in the company responsible for it – and put in enough time and resources to get things done.

First you must assess where you are now against the standard (available on the Investors in People website); then you will need to produce an action plan to identify priorities, targets, resources and timescales for achievement of recognition as an Investor in People*.

The national standard for effective investment in people

An Investor in People* makes a public commitment from the top to develop all employees to achieve its business objectives:

- Every employer should have a written but flexible plan which sets out business goals and targets, considers how employees will contribute to achieving the plan and specifies how development needs in particular will be assessed and met.
- Management should develop and communicate to all employees a vision of where the organisation is going and the contribution employees will make to its success, involving employee representatives as appropriate.

An Investor in People* regularly reviews the training and development needs of all employees:

- The resources for training and developing employees should be clearly identified in the business plan.
- Managers should be responsible for regularly agreeing training and development needs with each employee in the context of

business objectives, setting targets and standards linked, where appropriate, to the achievement of National Vocational Qualifications (or relevant units) and, in Scotland, Scottish Vocational Qualifications.

An Investor in People* takes action to train and develop individuals on recruitment and throughout their employment:

- Action should focus on the training needs of all new recruits and continually developing and improving the skills of existing employees.
- All employees should be encouraged to contribute to identifying and meeting their own job-related development needs.

An Investor in People* evaluates the investment in training and development to assess achievement and improve future effectiveness:

- The investment, the competence and commitment of employees, and the use made of skills learned, should be reviewed at all levels against business goals and targets.
- The effectiveness of training and development should be reviewed at the top level and lead to renewed commitment and target setting.

A CAREER DEVELOPMENT MODEL

A career development model within a nursery setting could look like Figure 4.2. This model does not imply that people can choose their jobs, but rather that the responsibility for putting themselves forward is theirs rather than just the manager's. If they are found to be ready to progress then they should be helped to prepare by the manager. If there is no higher job available to them, then they should be helped to broaden their experience while a suitable job is found.

To be effective and gain respect, an *appraisal system* must measure, debate and plan individual development and work targets, and generate useful feedback in both directions. It should:

- have a means of mutual discussion of past performance, present reality, and future opportunities and targets;
- relate to measurable work performance and target setting;

Managerial complexity	Manager
	Assessment point
	Senior management e.g. Deputy Manager
	Assessment point
	'Project' manager e.g. theme-planning
	Assessment point
	Supervision e.g. of NVQ candidates
	Assessment point
	Technical intake
	Time

FIGURE 4.2 Nursery management career model

- focus on observable behaviour rather than speculation on hazy queries of personal qualities;
- relate directly to individual pay packages;
- draw out training and development needs and contract to action on them;
- show next possible career steps and why;
- give an overview of likely ultimate career stage;
- have a fair appeal system.

The essence of such a system is the individual's performance in their job. This may seem an unnecessary statement, but many appraisals are more to do with the manager's personal views of the individual's characteristics. That approach short-changes the individual and has led to cases of 'undue care' being cited as a claim against employers.

The appraisal should be completed in pencil by both appraisee and appraiser before they meet, at which point they should agree a mutual scoring and a plan. Most people under-score themselves and have to be coaxed into agreeing a higher score.

The most successful appraisal systems start with measurable *performance indicators* of past work. They state targets, quality, resource usage, absences, etc., agreed at the previous appraisal and measure them against present reality.

The rating of *behaviour* is also fundamental to the appraisal system. Behaviours are observable and can be easily checked out if there is disagreement. 'Behaviours' are not 'characteristics', such as honesty, integrity, etc., which are highly subjective; they are directly related to the aims and style of the organisation. If you want a creative, responsive, customer-friendly, nurturing type of organisation, a measurable behaviour might be 'is seen to work well in all areas of the nursery' or 'is able to form effective working relationships with all members of the team'. If the words that resonate better are calm, methodical, judgemental type of organisation, you may consider that measurable behaviour such as 'is seen to make effective use of own/other people's time' is appropriate.

It has been found to be particularly powerful to involve staff in helping to agree the 'behaviours' for such a scheme. This has an energising effect and reinforces the shared culture of the organisation, as well as ensuring that people are committed to the appraisal process. The output from what are, typically, ten to twenty amenable behaviours can be plotted individually, and collectively, for feedback or trends in the organisation. In this way, the appraisal becomes part of *organisational learning*. The same behaviour with different targets should be capable of being used throughout the organisation.

From these measures of achievements and behaviours:

- new targets for the next period can be agreed;
- training and development needs can be identified and specified;
- next possible career steps can be discussed;
- concern about system/measurements can be taken forward, possibly to an identified 'external' appraiser.

There are several cost-effective ways of ensuring that personal development agreements are fulfilled. One is to use your staff as a training resource. Encourage staff to collect examples of development challenges and to share their observations at an informal meeting with those who organise training. The informality should also strengthen ties between centrally based and 'field' staff.

Another way is to increase staff commitment to the organisation by encouraging future senior staff to recruit new staff. This grants them a major responsibility while providing new staff with mentors who are not 'masters'.

Focus, too, on personnel relations. New members of staff should be greeted with a nursery manual, including basic information on management and administrations and quality-control expectations (see Chapter 2). Also, budget resources for educational activities. Every member of staff should be encouraged with a budget of time and money to take advantage of formal educational opportunities to maintain and develop existing skills. Encourage an awareness of new skills required, so that every member of staff is in a position to keep up to date with and initiate new ways of learning.

DELEGATING

In this section, the owner-manager is used by way of acknowledging that he/she probably incurs the greatest risks of *not* delegating. However, the advice applies to all in a management role. Remember, that you are not a leader unless you have followers, and appropriate delegation is the best possible way to grow your followers. Delegation does not change where ultimate responsibility lies for the financial control, the staff team and the reputation of the service, but it is absolutely clear that if you are trying to grow and develop the nursery, you will have more to communicate. Briefing groups are an excellent discipline for downward communication but there's a lot more to it than that. You need processes to ensure upward communication, and especially to coordinate across the organisation. So what is *your* best role and what must you look for in your deputy, administrative assistant, accountant, etc.?

Delegation – a remedy for overwork

Overwork is a common complaint of the small-business owner or manager: too much hard work and never enough hours in the day to do it. However, it is a problem that could easily be remedied by some effective delegation.

Delegation is simply the art of getting things done through other people. And if you show any of the following symptoms you should consider building delegating into the management of your business. Do you:

- have problems with deadlines for jobs that you do?
- have to work late regularly?
- take work home regularly?
- avoid accepting help with jobs?
- devote a lot of your time to details rather than planning and managing?

- feel insufficiently confident about your employees' ability to take on greater responsibility?

Delegation will help to keep the work flowing smoothly and so prevent a pile-up on your desk, which is both stress-inducing and counter-productive.

Fear of delegation

Most owner-managers are proud of the fact that they have built up their own company from nothing. In the beginning, entrepreneurs often perform all the tasks of running the business. This is reasonable enough, but as that operation grows they may hang on to too many jobs. They may believe that nobody else can do the job, and conversely it is just possible they may fear being shown up. It is also possible that, through pressure of work and the gradual nature of the expansion, they simply haven't reviewed the day-to-day management of their time.

Another reason for small-business owners not delegating is that sometimes the routine tasks are preferred to the difficult ones. Writing invoices is easier than preparing the new cash flow budget for the bank!

What has to be recognised is that when you delegate, both you and your employees get a chance to broaden skills. Through delegation you can ease your job of managing and thereby increase the effectiveness of both yourself and your staff – and thus your organisation.

Benefits for you

- *Delegation allows time to achieve more.* An owner-manager who can delegate effectively is likely to achieve greater output. Through the proper selection, assignment and coordination of tasks, a manager can mobilise resources to achieve more results than would have been possible without skilful delegation.
- *It allows time for managerial activities.* Delegation allows the owner-manager an opportunity to handle aspects of the job that no one else can do – project planning, plans for developing the business, monitoring how the business is doing, monitoring staff performance and dealing with any problems arising.

- *It provides you with back-up.* By delegating responsibility in different areas you will create a back-up workforce who can take over in times of emergency.

Benefits for staff

- *Delegation develops staff skills.* Owner-managers who fail to delegate effectively deprive staff of opportunities to improve their skills and assume greater responsibility. Since employees are likely to realise that they are not learning and gaining experience, they may well leave your organisation in order to find a more challenging and supportive environment. This happens most frequently with those staff who are most talented – precisely the people you least want to lose. What is a routine job for you is often a growth opportunity for a member of staff.
- *It increases staff involvement.* Proper delegation encourages others to participate more in understanding and influencing their work. By increasing their involvement in the workplace you will also increase their enthusiasm and initiative for their work.

Benefits for your organisation

- *Delegation maximises efficient output.* It does this by making the best use of available human resources so as to achieve the highest possible rate of productivity. It also provides the right environment for staff to offer new ideas that can improve the flow and operation of the workplace.
- *It produces faster and more effective decisions.* An organisation is most responsive to changes in the environment when individuals closest to the problems are making the decisions about resolving those problems.
- *It increases flexibility of operations.* Effective delegation trains several people to perform the same tasks. As a result, when someone is absent or when a crisis requires others to assist with functions not regularly a part of their job, several individuals will already be familiar with the assignment.
- *Delegation prepares people for promotion or rotation of responsibilities.* It supports concession planning.

Your five-point plan

1 Decide what and what not to delegate

The general guidelines for deciding what should be delegated are:

- the work can be handled accurately by your staff;
- all necessary information for decision-making is available to the individual being delegated the task;
- the task involves operational detail rather than planning;
- the task does not require skills unique to the manager's position;
- an individual other than you has, or can have, direct control over the tasks.

Therefore any routine jobs of information collection, or assignments involving extensive detail such as making calculations, are things that can be delegated. Tasks that should *not* be delegated include the delegation process itself, employee appraisal and discipline, planning and forecasting, confidential tasks, complex situations and sensitive situations.

2 Decide to whom to delegate

Obviously your ability to delegate will be governed by the size and quality of your staff team at any given time. However, three factors are of primary importance when selecting the right person for an assignment: (a) their skills, (b) their interest and (c) their work-load.

3 Communicate your decision

Describe what it is you are delegating and give the other person enough information to carry out the task. Presenting the directive in writing will prevent the 'I didn't know' syndrome. If a gap exists between the assignment and an employee's skills you must be very clear and concise in describing the steps of the task.

Bear in mind that a new assignment, particularly one involving several stages, is unlikely to be completely understood on the first explanation. Make yourself available for further clarification as the staff member works through the assignment; close monitoring will save time in the long run.

4 Manage and evaluate

From the beginning, clearly establish set times when you will meet with the person to review their performance. The secret of delegation is to follow up.

5 Reward

Results that are recognised get repeated. You must monitor and respond to the person's performance. Otherwise it's like playing a game without keeping score, which in the end is not motivating.

Starting to delegate

Part of the essence of delegation is thoughtfully judging when a new employee is ready to handle a more stimulating assignment. If necessary delegate in stages, starting with small tasks and working up to more challenging projects.

Of course, the one thing you can never delegate is accountability. No matter who handles the task, as the manager it's your reputation that is on the line.

Delegation is a form of risk-taking, so if you cannot deal with a few mistakes you will never be able to delegate. Nonetheless, effective delegation that is carefully planned and well executed will result in a freeing-up of your time and a more efficient organisation.

A summary checklist for effective delegation is included as an appendix to this chapter.

RECRUITING STAFF

Getting the right people is a difficult, time-consuming and costly business. Getting it wrong is even more expensive and can be extremely painful. Few growing businesses can claim not to have fallen into this trap. However, you can increase the odds on success by putting in place some basic processes and disciplines:

- Decide on the *numbers and skills mix* you are going to need over the next one to three years.
- Prepare *job descriptions* covering job titles and purpose, to whom responsible, limits of accountability and main tasks.

- Prepare a *person specification* outlining the sort of person you think is likely to be effective in the job. This is particularly important to explore the candidate's attitude and fit with the team.
- *Source your requirements creatively,* through networks of contacts and employment agencies, and looking at others' advertisements for staff.
- *Design and place an advertisement* that explains the nursery/organisation's unique differences.
- *Weed out* application forms or CVs of those who don't fit the job description and person specification.
- *Invite* the candidates chosen for interview to make an informal visit to the nursery prior to interview, to see their potential place of work and to spend time with established staff. This will stimulate questions they can ask at their interview.
- *Collect* first impressions made by staff when candidate visited.

Forty-five seconds, it is claimed, is the time a typical manager takes from meeting an applicant before deciding whether or not he or she is the right person for the job. True or false, fears that the interview can be very subjective, and thus a biased way of selecting staff, are promoting the trend for companies to use standard measurement principles – such as those above – when recruiting.

APPENDIX TO CHAPTER 4: EFFECTIVE DELEGATION

Principles

- Careful selection of jobs or assignments to delegate
- A clear view of the boundary between effective delegation and complete abdication
- Detailed planning and establishment of priorities
- Knowledge of delegate's capabilities, characteristics and experience
- Selection of proper delegate
- Establishment of goals and objectives for delegated tasks
- An understanding and agreement on standards of performance
- Provision for support as needed (volunteered and requested)
- Assessment of results and correction of errors
- Encouragement of independence
- Rewards or recognition where justified

- Acceptance by delegator of methods other than his/her own
- Establishment of trust and mutual understanding

Obstacles to delegation

- Inability of delegate to handle job (actual inability)
- Lack of confidence in delegate (perceived inability) in judgement, attitude, respect of others, etc.
- Fear of competition from delegate
- Exposure of weakness in delegator
- Lack of time for instructions and training
- Wish of delegator to do the particular job him/herself
- Belief by delegator that s/he is delegating adequately
- Perfectionism

Obstacles to acceptance of delegation by subordinate

- It is often easier to ask the boss than work it through
- Fear of criticism, especially when it is not fully warranted
- Lack of necessary information
- Lack of adequate resources
- Lack of self-confidence
- Lack of adequate incentive
- A feeling that the boss always wants his/her own way on what is done

Delegation usually works best when:

- delegate is physically distant;
- delegator is absent frequently;
- workloads are heavy;
- there are many tight deadlines;
- the organisation is young and vigorous with the emphasis on problem-solving;
- standards of performance are attainable and fair;
- the delegator feels personally secure;
- a favourable environment exists which emphasises development, growth, innovation, creativity and human dignity;
- a great deal of mutual trust exists at all levels of the organisation.

Chapter 5

Being an ambassador

- Philosophy
- Philosophy determines priorities
- Promoting the nursery
- Questions parents ask
- Working with parents
- Networking
- Appendix

PHILOSOPHY

A major report in 1990 (Rumbold, 1990)* noted that the aims of the curriculum will be most readily achieved where skilled and knowledgeable staff have high expectations of children, and value parents as their child's first educator and as active partners in the continuing process of education. These principles were embedded in the Children Act, and *Every Child Matters** builds on and consolidates the centrality of parents, carers and families to a young child's start in life at nursery. The NICHD* study in the US, as well as EPPE* in the UK have found that family characteristics are an important factor in children's progress, in particular, parent engagement in the pre-school setting attended.

The high profile that early years services have enjoyed over the past ten years, both in public policy and the press, as well as a raft of 'how to choose childcare' booklets have informed and equipped parents to articulate what they seek in a nursery. They now recognise the importance of a nursery having principles and expect them to shine through the delivery of the service. The connection between child development theory and practice has been clarified through many helpful guides. Thanks to campaigning groups such as Working Families, parents also understand work–life balance issues, and as an increasing number of parents seek flexible work – and require similar understanding of their situation and flexibility from the nursery.

It is now usual for nurseries to have a policy on organic and/or locally produced food, and on recycling in the nursery. These issues are not only important to parents themselves but also in relation to the attitudes and habits the children will pick up from adults in the nursery. It is crucial that the nursery is realistic about the extent to which it is going to make a guarantee about its commitment to such rapidly developing aspects of our lives.

It is often more difficult for many nursery staff to articulate philosophy. If a nursery follows a particular recognised vocational philosophy (e.g. Montessori, Steiner, Froebel) it may be reasonably straightforward to articulate, and parents will recognise what you are talking about. However, most do not, because their starting point is *not* that of a school but of a new provision – the dedicated under-fives provision for parents who have a choice. It is more likely that the nursery has drawn on a number of sources and developed a hybrid philosophy (see Figure 5.1).

The nursery's philosophy is its marketing offer. And what is most essential to the owner of the nursery is that each and every staff member

- Goldschmied and Jackson: Working from what children can do (physical competence) and how they think. 'I can . . .', 'I know . . .'
- Weikart *et al.* (High/Scope): Children learning from real experiences and progressing to abstract signs; stages of representation through 'key experiences', towards understanding
- Malaguzzi, Italy: Towards communicating the 100 languages of children
- Athey/Bruce/Nutbrown/Kellog: Schema; threads of thinking; patterns of play; persistent cognitive concerns
- Denmark (The Forest Nursery): Learning in the open air; children learning about the natural world and using it for their play

FIGURE 5.1 Some examples of working models

should ooze it. Very few parents will choose a nursery unseen, or on its literature alone.

Parents are the market. Nursery staff are ambassadors for the service in reaching that market. The perspective of parents is the external rationale for nursery nurses to appreciate the philosophy and approach of the setting they work in. But there are internal reasons as well.

PHILOSOPHY DETERMINES PRIORITIES

Some nurseries may be concerned with the order and pace of the day: everyone knowing what is expected of them and when; how long institutional functions should take; and how many activities and of what variety should take place each day. Others may consider that if a group of children is enjoying a particular activity, it doesn't matter that they are 'late' for tea.

All will have invested resources carefully, and it may be that the smooth running of the nursery relies on each activity being properly cleared away before the next one starts. Is it OK then, within the team, for one person to be allocated to sit and play with the expectant children, or should everyone be involved in clearing up so that everyone can move on together?

Harmony in the team is built on shared philosophies, mutual understanding and respect for why things are run as they are. In order to join the team, the nursery nurse must establish what he or she needs to know *before* starting, on the *first day* and during the *first few weeks*.

Before starting

'How is the nursery explained to parents?', 'Can I sign up to the philosophies as they are expressed?', 'Can I accept that the way we do things is . . .?'

Being a manager means being able to share and promote the aspirations of the organisation, both internally and externally. Before taking on the role, it is important that you know where you stand on, for example, group care as distinct from one-to-one attention; babies in nurseries; the length of the nursery day; discipline of young children; taking young children into the workplace; the difference between a nursery, a nursery school, a playgroup, etc. It is reasonable that both staff and parents rely on you as a manager to articulate the philosophy of the organisation and believe it! Parents, particularly first-time parents, are anxious about all these issues, possibly do not know where they stand on many of them, and require constant reassurance that they are not leading their child along the wrong path.

It is equally important that staff can accept the way in which the nursery's philosophy is articulated to children: 'The way we behave towards each other in nursery is. . .'. This will usually involve a particular approach to equal opportunities, to the format and flow of the nursery day, and to the extent to which children of differing ages are grouped together. How strongly do you feel that, despite the cultural background of the child that may suggest a different approach in nursery, mealtimes are relaxed, social occasions? Or, how important is it that all children have the opportunity to access all core areas of activity every day? To what extent should four-year-olds be protected from the boisterous toddlers?

How familiar can staff be with parents? Who speaks to them about what? At what point is a member of staff expected to intervene in a child's activity? These are just some of the crucial things to get right on your first day as a manager, which means that you need to explore them before you begin.

It is important to know how the hierarchy and roles within the staff team work, and how each individual can influence the quality of service. Equally important is to know how the pattern might be upset. This is discussed in Chapter 4.

The first few weeks

Increasingly, you will be expected to explain and discuss with parents the nursery's viewpoint on all the foregoing issues. The areas for misunderstanding on the part of parents are numerous, and this – coupled with the level of detail about which parents expect to be informed – requires scrupulous attention to consistency on the part of staff. It is neither helpful nor fair to parents to have two differing versions of, for example, the nursery's discipline policy.

On their first visit, parents will want to see and feel:

- a welcoming atmosphere;
- children taking positive pride in their work and play;
- positive relationships between staff/children, children/children, staff/staff;
- positive documentation – what is being achieved;
- positive autonomy of staff – staff empowered and supported to make the appropriate decisions;
- positive awareness of the manager, and your familiarity with all current issues in the nursery;
- positive planning of activities – evidence that staff are proactive and take a real interest in the construction of a current programme for the children;
- positive expectations of children.

The Inner London Education Authority *Junior School Project* (1980)* identified that parents looked for signs, when visiting nurseries and primary schools, that would lead to their children:

'doing as well as possible'
'being happy and enjoying it'
'learning to be polite and well-behaved'
'reading and writing as soon as possible'.

Being an effective ambassador for the nursery is about describing the features of the nursery service in terms that parents can understand, appreciate and desire. Even though the academic underpinning for the service, and the motivation of the 'driving force', is probably why you took on the job, it is the translation of these into real benefits for the parents that will achieve your real goal – a full and thriving nursery. This translation process is detailed in Chapter 6. However, it is worth pausing here to consider the factors that have been found to be critical in achieving the outcomes for parents identified above (see Figure 5.2). They provide an agenda for review by the new manager.

PROMOTING THE NURSERY

Promotion is a catch-all word for marketing communications: advertising, personal selling, sales promotions and public relations. Doing business without promotion, it has been said, is like working in the dark: you know what you are doing but no one else does!

But promotion is probably the most intangible area of expenditure in a nursery business. Discovering exactly what benefits you get from the money you spend is a problem that taxes most business people. Lord Leverhulme, the founder of the soaps and detergents empire Lever Brothers, is reputed to have said 'I know half the money I spend on advertising is wasted. The problem is to know which half.'

Budgets are always tight in nurseries. If there is anything to spare, of course you want to spend it on improving the service – something of direct benefit to the children. A method of advertising needs to be chosen that you will get through to most of your likely parent group at least cost. Remember also that you do not generate bookings directly from advertising; it simply initiates that process, raises awareness of your particular service in the selected market. Bookings are made only once the advertising has taken effect and parents come to visit. There are a number of issues to be decided.

- Purposeful leadership
- Involvement of all staff in management
- Consistency of approach and methods amongst staff
- Planned and purposeful sessions
- Challenging teaching
- Work-centred environments
- Children's opportunity for debate
- Maximum communication between children and adults
- Up-to-date record-keeping
- Parental involvement
- Positive approach to improvement/development

FIGURE 5.2 Factors critical to the effectiveness of a nursery

Segmenting the market: who are you trying to attract?

What type of parent is going to share your interests and aspirations for young children, and where are they located? Do they belong to identifiable socio-economic groups, or do they need to, in terms of your fee structure? Your advertising choices must follow from the answers to these questions. Are you just looking to fill the nursery from your immediate local area, or is it a central point that parents pass through – on their way to work, for instance? Should you also then be looking at where they come from?

Setting advertising objectives: what are you asking parents to do?

Do you want them to ring you, visit the nursery, think again about nurseries versus nannies? The message must convey the response you expect the parents to make. You may believe that what you want to do is raise awareness of how your nursery differs from others, in the hope that parents will retain the message until they need to *use* the information. On the other hand, you may be issuing an invitation to visit the nursery for a specific purpose. It is useful to pinpoint precisely what is intended. Do you want to:

- increase telephone enquiries by say 10 per cent over 6 months?
- raise awareness of the nursery in a previously untargeted residential area?
- generate an additional (say) twenty visits to the nursery before Christmas?

Defining the advertising message: what should you say?

Look at the nursery service from the parents' standpoint and answer the hypothetical question, 'Why should I book a place in your nursery?' It is best to consider the answer in two stages:

- 'Why should I book a place in *any* nursery?' What benefits will nursery care have over, say, nanny, childminder or a nursery class?

- 'Why should I book a place in *your* nursery?' What advantages does your nursery have for me, over others?

Having said all that, the most effective form of advertising is the kind that existing parents do for you, by recommending your service to friends. Staying in touch with your present parents' wishes is a large element of your advertising plan, because it provides you with the information for what *they* want to hear, and pass on.

Deciding on the creative angle: how do we deliver the message?

Possibly the most important point to remember here is that you should not choose the medium *you* like best, but the one that is most appropriate (see Figure 5.3).

Not all methods of communication carry an equal impact. It has already been noted that by far the most effective form of advertising is that of a recommendation of a trusted friend. Here is a summary of the best uses of various other forms:

- Leaflets give a short, memorable, personal message.
- Newspapers can deliver longer, more complex, one-off messages.
- Magazines deliver highly targeted, complex messages.
- Radio and television convey short repeated messages.
- Outdoor billboards carry short, high-impact messages.
- Indoor billboards carry more detailed, subtle messages.
- Transport interiors can have long, complex messages.
- Transport exteriors carry short, high-impact messages.

Straight facts	Yellow Pages, Thomsons, etc.
Reasoning	Advert or article logically explaining the benefits of the nursery
Emotions	Advert associating the nursery with pleasant connotations or mood, or peace of mind
Hard sell	Advert commands action: 'Nurseries are good for you'
Endorsement	Advert uses role models: 'Snow White uses our nursery'

FIGURE 5.3 Choosing the medium for promotion

Setting the advertising budget: how much should you spend?

The 'What can we afford?' approach implies that advertising is an extravagance. Given what we know about the effects of occupancy levels on all aspects of service, this approach must be questioned.

A more logical approach is to look at how much you have been spending, and relate it to how you feel about occupancy. That is, if you spent 5 per cent of total income last year and you are maintaining occupancy levels as intended, then there is little reason to suppose it needs changing.

The cost/benefit approach takes this one step further. If you reckon that a £250 advertisement 'cost' will generate 25 enquiries, and you know that 10 per cent of enquiries generally turn into bookings, and you have the staffing, etc. in place to accept the additional children, in this case 2.5, then the 'benefit' to you is the profit margin on 2.5 places. This will provide you with some guidance on whether a particular advertising cost is worthwhile.

Measuring the results

Because advertising is expensive it is important to monitor the results of everything you do, and not to repeat wasted effort. Figure 5.4 shows how this could be done.

Such an analysis will help you to understand not only what enquiries are most likely to turn into bookings, but also how relatively expensive different forms of advertising are, and which are better used for raising general awareness of the nursery, and which for immediate bookings.

Getting ready

The nursery should look at its best and staff should be prepared for the family you are receiving. This means that you need to collect as much information about the family before they visit. Is the parent returning to work? Is their child the only one? Cleanliness and a tidy nursery say a great deal about your attention to detail and are basic concerns of parents, as they relate directly to the health and safety of their child. Staff should know the age of the child who the parent is considering placing in the nursery, in order that they can prepare for the priorities that the parent will have. If the parent is looking for a baby place, then a calm and peaceful atmosphere is important, alongside a generous (but realistic) staff quota

	Local news-paper	Leaflets	Posters	Personal recommen-dation	Total
Cost	£200	£100	£1,000	£0	£1,300
Telephone enquiries	50	30	100	10	190
Cost per enquiry	£4	£3.33	£10	£0	£6.84
Visits	5	20	20	10	55
Cost per visit	£40	£5	£50	£0	£23.64
Bookings	2	5	3	5	15
Cost per booking	£100	£20	£333	£0	£86.67

FIGURE 5.4 Measuring the results of advertising

to provide as much individual attention as possible. If the child is over 2 years, then the parent is more likely to be concerned about and questioning around their preparation for school, how friendships are fostered and activity planning.

Involving staff in the conversation with parents and inviting the parent to spend time, say, in the baby room will give them lasting insights into the way you work and confidence, at a time when they are likely to feel quite vulnerable, in the depth and continuity in the staff team. Some years ago, one of Nurseryworks' nurseries participated in the testing of a research instrument being used by Penelope Leach, for the *Families Children and Childcare Study** (ongoing). Early findings from the study show that mothers today rank the 'communicative variables' as of greater importance than other aspects of a nursery, with 'a loving and understanding environment' as their number one priority. This suggests that parents have come to terms with the idea that their young child can get attached to a carer, and that this is positive.

Most parents can be expected to be aware of *Birth to Three Matters**, the Government's curriculum framework for the youngest children. This has four aspects:

- a strong child;
- a skilful communicator;
- a competent learner;
- a healthy child.

The framework recognises that children have from birth a need to develop, learn and explore the world around them. This framework now forms part of the regulatory process and nurseries will be expected to show how their own planning and delivery responds to *Birth to Three Matters**.

Many nurseries are tucked away, and proper attention to providing good directions, and information about who the parent will meet, together with an invitation to stay awhile and observe, will all suggest you are confident about what you offer, and open to building a strong relationship from the outset.

What exactly are you selling?

Having attracted parents to visit the nursery, how do you ensure that they collect all the information they need to make a decision to book a place?

A *passive* approach would be to describe what goes on in each area of the nursery, and allow the parent to take in as much as they could about nursery life.

A more *proactive* approach would be to consider what it is that your nursery offers over and above other nurseries, and to find a way of ensuring that the parent leaves in full knowledge of the benefits these features bring.

What are the components of the sales package? Firstly, the *service* itself:

- what it does and what it consists of;
- what children get out of it;
- what parents get out of it.

Increasingly, as parents seek financial help from their employers, a further bullet would read:

- What the parent's employer will get out of it.

The way the service is described will be informed by what you know about the needs and aspirations of parents, and what knowledge and views you have on the way children develop.

It is important that the service be described in a way that the parent can understand. For example, if you have an organisational structure in which a group of children pursue individual academic goals through collaborative efforts, why not say that: 'Children learn and play in small groups around an activity that they have chosen.'

What you think makes the nursery special may actually be meaningless to the parent who is rarely an early years specialist, and it needs to be *translated* (see Figure 5.5). For instance, the staff ratio may be higher in your nursery than in others, or your staff team may be better qualified. You can deduce from this that your service is above average in quality, but saying that does not really do anything for the parent. If, however, the parent can see these aspects of your service as contributing to a better educational start for their child, then the message has been received.

QUESTIONS PARENTS ASK

In my experience, there are a number of concerns that parents express, time and time again. The following represents a selection of answers that may be helpful:

Q 'Why choose the nursery option? How can group care ever be better than the one-to-one attention of a nanny or childminder?'

Answer: 'Practically speaking, nurseries provide continuity. Nurseries don't get ill, go on holiday or hand in their notice. More important is the child's emotional stability. If a child is intensely attached to a single carer and that person then leaves for whatever reason, the experience can be deeply traumatic. Multiply that experience a few times and a child may become wary of making any attachments at all.

Features	Benefits to child	Parents' impression
Above-average quality of service	Best start in life for child	Good parenting decision
Professional management	Reliable and financially stable	Value for money
Constantly developing/ innovative on service	Adapting to child's and parents' changing and individual needs	State-of-the-art purchase

FIGURE 5.5 Examples of translating features into benefits

'A related issue is the jealousy and emotional conflict that some parents feel if their child becomes deeply devoted to the nanny to the exclusion of themselves. Our nurseries provide a dependable, secure environment which complements rather than supplants the parents' role. The confidence children acquire at nursery is broad-based, not contingent on a single relationship.

'The positive benefits of nursery care are far-reaching. By engaging in a group, children learn to respect others, to be aware of each others' needs, to share, take turns and cooperate in creative play and activity. All of these skills help to foster the development of language and communication, as children learn to interact with each other and those who look after them.

'A good nursery meets objective, measurable standards. Parents can see the quality of care that is offered and trust their choice to a far greater extent than if they were placing their child in the hands of just one person.'

Q 'What about babies? Should babies be cared for in nurseries at all?'

Answer: 'Babies can and do flourish in a nursery environment, provided certain conditions are met. Babies have the ability to develop attachments with several people, but not with many people. For this reason, we take care to select and keep staff with the maturity and instinctive warmth to form close bonds with small babies and their parents – carers who are able to put the needs of babies first and follow their lead when it comes to play, activity and routine.

'The areas within nurseries specifically designed for babies offer calm, peaceful and stimulating surroundings where they can begin to explore the world.

'We know parents want their babies to be the focus of loving attention and this is what we provide.'

Q What is your attitude to discipline?

Answer: 'Recent research shows that this issue is of particular concern to parents of toddlers! This isn't surprising, since the toddler's desire for independence, knowledge and control over their world can often clash with the fact that they are still largely dependent on adults to make things happen.

 130

'Confining children within a rigid set of imposed rules does little to foster true self-control. Our staff expect the best – not the worst – of the children in our care. Good manners, sociable behaviour, fairness and kindness all stem from a basic awareness of the needs of others, and every two-year-old needs support and encouragement to take this huge conceptual step. By promoting the core values of respect and self-esteem, sharing and participation, the nursery worker can guide the child through this challenging phase of development.

'Of course, behaviour that is harmful to the child or to others can never be tolerated or accepted. But understanding the reason for a tantrum or temperamental outburst, talking it through calmly with the child, proposing alternatives, are all part of the process of helping the child gain a better command of their emotions and show a positive response to others.'

Q 'What provision do you make for pre-school children? Wouldn't this age group be better served in a nursery class at school?'

Answer: 'There is still a distinction between nurseries and nursery schools, and it has a lot to do with the environment. What we aim to offer here is a blend of care and education that secures young children as confident and independent learners. We approach young children's learning from where each individual child is at the moment, and extend their learning at a pace they can cope with and enjoy. This instils learning skills and high self-esteem, so that when they do reach school, they do not flounder, and have the emotional and social capabilities to permit them to thrive.

'Here, you will not find a mini-classroom that stems from "teaching", rather than "learning", and set up formally. Number work and reading and writing will not happen at fixed times in the day or week and will not rely on one teacher being present. However, you will find a structured programme of choices for children, all of which have been carefully planned to meet the learning needs of each child and designed, first and foremost, to stir their curiosity and hold their attention. Numbers and words permeate everything we do, and through conversation between child and adult, the connections are made. Look at some of our displays to see how this works in our activities. Our curriculum is linked with the *Early Years Foundation Stage**, so we can see and compare how our children fare as compared with those working towards the same learning outcomes in schools. The principal difference is that we are entirely focused on the needs of young children.'

Q 'Your nursery is located in the City. What can young children gain by accompanying their parents to work?'

Answer: 'Time is precious to working parents. Bringing children into the City, close to where you work, can make good use of what would otherwise be empty commuting time. Travelling in by train, bus or car offers the opportunity to share stories, songs – or just talk. A nursery near your office means you are close at hand – to share lunch with your child, join in birthday celebrations and activities – fathers, too! You are also nearby in the case of illness, or if extra demands at work disrupt your normal schedule.

'The City nursery provides all the resources of home-based care – libraries, swimming pools, parks and shops – with the important advantage that your child is included within the framework of your working world.'

Q 'Your nurseries are relatively expensive. Isn't there any way of cutting costs?'

Answer: 'The short answer is no. We are dedicated to quality, surpassing the high standards laid down in legislation in every field – safety, educational provision, diet, outside activity and the design and equipping of our nursery spaces. But the highest proportion of our overhead goes on staff. There is no way of trimming costs without compromising our central philosophy, the nursery worker–child ratio, the level of dedication, effort and continuity we expect and achieve from those we employ.'

Q 'How does nursery care benefit children in the long term? Is it the best start in life?'

Answer: 'Many studies suggest that nursery experience gives the child a flying start. Children who have been exposed to a wider social group and mix at an early age are generally better equipped to work in a team, to cooperate and share, and form good friendships and working partnerships during their years of formal schooling. Evidence suggests that they also go on to do better in terms of educational achievement, in the acquisition of reading, writing and numerical skills.

'All parents want the best for their children, and all parents want their children to achieve. But the desire for children to progress and perform must never be gained at the expense of their emotional needs. A child is only a child once. We believe in helping children realise their potential within a secure framework of care and support. The best start you can give your children is measured not only by their future prowess but in the quality of their daily experience now, in their present happiness, well-being and zest for life. This, essentially, is what we mean by putting the child first.

'At our nursery we respond to children. We take care to promote physical well-being, to stimulate development of new skills and to meet emotional needs.

'Teamwork is the cornerstone of our policy. We take care to select the best staff – to choose those who are bright, aware and enthusiastic – to build a community committed to the support of both parents and children.

'Children deserve the best environment to flourish and play in safety. We take care to design spaces that children enjoy, to equip and maintain our nurseries to the highest standard, to build in opportunities for exploration and discovery – to make children feel at home.

'A good environment also means stable routines and core values. We take care to balance activity with nurture, to foster sharing and participation, to encourage social interplay and individual expression, to build confidence and promote self-esteem.

'The early years represent a most intense period of growth and development in a child's life. Our expertise is founded on interaction with parents and children, thorough appraisal of the latest developments in educational thinking, and constant re-evaluation of needs and aims. We put your children first – because you do.'

Parents will also require more specific information about aspects of the nursery service. You must decide what your service priorities are. Here I offer my own, as a starting point.

Quality of care

The key-worker system

'Each child is assigned a key-worker with personal responsibility for overseeing progress and maintaining continuity. Children need a focus, a special person to whom to relate. Our key-worker system provides a dependable relationship to ease times of transition at the beginning and end of the day.'

Feedback

'Our staff are trained to make detailed observations of your child's progress. Friendly and responsive, they will always make time to share details of your child's daily achievements and activities, and respond to your concerns. Children delight in displaying their triumphs, from messing about with paint to using the potty unaided. Noticeboards provide an essential backup, displaying artwork, menus, news and information about activities.'

Environment

'Our nurseries have been specifically designed and equipped to provide a stimulating, child-centred environment which combines the friendly atmosphere of home with the opportunities to explore and widen experience. We use natural materials whenever we can source them, and ensure that we maximise the recycling opportunities available to us from our local authority.'

Food

'Mealtimes are important moments in the day. All meals are freshly prepared and cooked on the premises, taking into account specific cultural and dietary needs. Staff and children sit down together to eat in small family groups. We source as much food from our immediate local area as we can, and we only use organic vegetables, fruit, meat, fish and dairy products.'

Rest

'We ensure activity is balanced with regular periods of rest. Routine naps, periods of quiet activity and shared stories mean the child is not overtired, fretful or anxious at the end of the day. Variety of experience makes children eager to learn, while a familiar framework of orderly routines shapes the day and provides stability.'

Safety

'All our nurseries are regularly inspected and surpass the exacting standards required by current legislation. Our staff are fully trained in emergency and first aid procedures.'

Learning together

Following the child

'The open-plan nursery layout is organised to provide different centres of activity from which each child is free to choose. We believe in following and supporting the child's focus of interest, and respecting their choices, not directing or enforcing attention. Children may be invited to participate in shared activities, but never compelled.'

Exploration and discovery

'Children investigate the world through all the senses – touch, taste, smell, sight and sound – and in the process discover exciting new concepts – heavy and light, before and after, high and low. By broadening the realm of experience we provide the opportunity to explore and experiment. To a child, an educational toy can be a bunch of keys, a sponge, a ball of wool, a funny hat, a bucket of sand, a string of beads – everyday items that can serve as vehicles for the acquisition of new manipulative and cognitive skills.'

Stages

'Babies start by exploring you and themselves, then greedily seize the world of colour and shape and texture, learning through focused attention and observation. Toddlers love to copy and mimic and need role models for their boisterous activity. Through dismantling and constructing they test the limits of their world and begin to learn independence. Pre-school children are ready to share and respond to the challenge of teamwork and activities that extend their concentration. Our child-centred programmes are designed to respond to each child individually and support their own path of development.'

Structured programme

'The role of the nursery worker is to facilitate learning experience, to engage with the child and support emerging skills and interests. It looks like play – and it is – play with a purpose. We offer a wealth of different activities to provide a fresh and challenging environment for discovery and fun. Each activity is planned to ensure it offers the potential to challenge children at different levels of development.'

Language

'Language is the key to learning. Names and labels, songs, stories and rhymes promote literacy and verbal fluency. Group care brings wider exposure to language and fosters communication skills.'

Consultation

'Our nursery programmes are the result of a constant process of refinement and development. Consultation with childcare and education professionals informs our thinking and practice. Just as important, we listen to parents to find out what they want for their children. Regular get-togethers enable everyone to share their views and initiate new approaches.'

Terms and conditions

The second part of what you are selling is the contract to which you are asking parents to commit. It is vital that parents read and understand the essential points before they book a place. Do not underestimate the damage that can be done to relations with parents, quite apart from the business, of terms and conditions of contract not being properly understood.

Of course, the last thing parents want to hear when they are delighted to have found your nursery, and decide to book a place, are the rather negative-sounding messages contained in 'notice periods' and 'deposits'. However, there is no substitute for being crystal clear about these issues from the outset. In particular, make sure that parents understand the following:

- deposit arrangements;
- fees;

- payment terms;
- notice of withdrawal period.

The appendix to this chapter contains specimen 'terms and conditions'.

Help with payment

A nursery manager will be expected to be familiar with the many schemes that are now available to help parents pay for early years provision. These include the Nursery Education Grant*, administered through local authorities, and the *Working Families Tax Credit**, administered through HMRC (HM Revenue and Customs*), and mainly targeted at lower income families and intended to provide choice to parents. They should also understand the incentives in place to assist employers to help parents with childcare costs. These include tax-efficient *Childcare Vouchers**, and workplace nurseries, both of which are usually offered to employees through salary sacrifice or salary top-up schemes, approved by HMRC for tax exemption purposes. Daycare Trust has produced a useful guide to these schemes, which can be found at www.daycaretrust.org.uk. It is important for managers to keep up to date with changes, usually introduced as part of the Government's Budget in April each year, so that they can advise a prospective parent to discuss the matter with their employer with a view to getting help with childcare costs.

WORKING WITH PARENTS

Combining work and family

The most successful childcare strategies for working parents lie at the intersection of employer challenges, working parents' needs and community enrichment (see Figure 5.6).

The majority of parents who choose to use private nurseries are working. This is because very often a private nursery is the only group provision available to them, but also this form of provision has become popular with working parents because its focus is on providing a service that is flexible to their needs as well as reflecting their aspirations for their child.

The early twenty-first century has brought a plethora of reports that have raised the profile of work–life balance, largely as a reflection of the

137

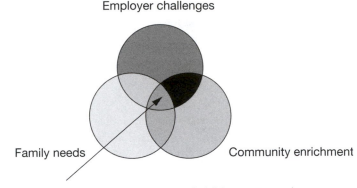

Employer challenges

Family needs

Community enrichment

The most successful employer-sponsored child care strategies lie at the intersection of employer challenges, working parents' needs and community enrichment.

FIGURE 5.6 The meeting point

'long hours' culture at work so prevalent in the UK, and the stress that this imposes, most clearly on mothers who work. An important contribution to the debate was published by Working Families in 2004, *Time, Health and the Family**, and in 2006, *Is Less More?** This report warned of the dangers of extended schools provision turning into more hours of childcare demanded by parents. These concerns have led to a high demand for flexible work, mirrored by part-time nursery places. The sector has had difficulty responding to this change, evidenced by a government consultation in 2005 that suggested that one in four parents cited a mismatch of childcare hours to working hours as one of their top three concerns around childcare, given the inevitable voids it leaves in nursery places. However, it is a trend which is only going to increase, and providers need to re-think their business models to provide the real flexibility that parents want today. The new focus on work–life balance has driven an increase in maternity leave from 6 to 9 months (2007), and a goal has been set down by the Government to extend this to 12 months from the end of the next Parliament. Within the same timescale parents are also to have the right to transfer a proportion of their maternity leave and pay to fathers. It would be ironic for the early years sector to encourage a pattern of working that goes against the flow of public perception around the way parents of young children should work to preserve a work–life balance.

138

All this has focused the minds of those parents who wish to combine a career with bringing up a family on the relationship between quality and cost.

Nursery and parents as partners

Once, it would have been close to heresy to equate the needs of the child's family with those of the child within a nursery service. But today there is greater understanding that children do not appear at nursery alone; that improving outcomes for children necessarily involves their family. This does not conflict with the child remaining at the centre of the service offered, but it is more inclusive and sensitive to what their future ability to thrive depends on. Nursery can only fill one pair of these shoes.

There is no substitute for giving parents the opportunity to experience at first hand how their children will spend their day and the benefits that the nursery environment will bring to the children. As much time as possible should be afforded to the parents to enable them to feel happy and positive about the nursery environment, and to ensure that they are introduced to each aspect of the nursery service. We have found that, should a problem arise at a later date, it can invariably be traced back to the parent not having been made aware of that particular procedure or approach, either because the settling was rushed or for the lack of opportunity to experience nursery life.

Working parents are a transitory population and turnover of parents in the nursery will be high. This means that, although it is important for parents to have an overview of the whole service offered by the nursery, it is equally important that they be reminded of the next phase of the service as their child prepares for it. If they join when their child is a baby then their greatest concerns and interest will be with the baby unit, its staff and routines. Although parents will acknowledge and hear your explanation of the changes in the curriculum as a child develops and grows, they will probably not be so questioning as those who are entering their child at two years. So, settling is not just a once-off process; it must be followed up and parents resettled at each phase-change.

It should now be regarded as normal practice in nurseries for parents to be welcomed into the nursery at any time of day, to observe or to take part in activities with their child and others. Working parents frequently find themselves precluded from this because of the pattern of their working day, so that contact is limited to arrival and collection times. Interestingly, some nurseries in the City of London report more lunchtime visits from parents, especially fathers, than nurseries in regional or residential locations, because the nurseries are adjacent to the worksite. Some years ago, where the employer provided a workplace nursery, there was concern around being seen visiting your child during working hours, but workplace nurseries are now a source of pride to most employers who have set them up. The employer wants to demonstrate that they are taking work–life balance seriously.

Actively encouraging parents to get involved in story telling and outings with other children, as well as their own, pays dividends in terms of their understanding and support for what the nursery does. If they have any special talents, such as playing a musical instrument, a craft, or have connections with another country or culture, they are usually very happy to share it in a session with children and staff. A parents' notice board can display current childcare-related clippings from the press and local events, and requests for special resources to support activities. Bright daily diary displays are a useful way of giving parents a snapshot of what has gone on that day, and what they can expect the next day, and individual notes on every child's experience complete the information a parent needs to stay in touch. However, no written information can take the place of a personal handover with a member of staff, at both meet and greet time. This allows follow-up on observations made of the child, which will contribute to the child's development profile and is particularly important for babies who develop dramatically in a short period of time.

Organised parents' sessions are usually welcomed, but for busy people such events need to respond to a real need on the part of the parents or the nursery, so that time can be set aside to attend. We have found that occasional social events with staff are popular. However, parents network anyway and many longlasting friendships between parents have been born in the nursery quite informally. We have also found that parents welcome information about child development and help with the choices they must make as their child grows. The most successful parents' sessions we have held have been where an expert speaker has led discussion on an identified parental concern, such as choosing a school, early childhood illnesses and early literacy. Such events provide the nursery with the added opportunity to remind parents of nursery policy as well as to hear current parents' views.

Steering groups

Many nurseries have steering groups or consultation groups, which are used as a forum for reviewing policy and contributing new ideas. These usually meet regularly throughout the year and can be a very important means of ensuring that the nursery does not become an island, limited by its own daily experiences. The membership of such a Group needs to be carefully considered alongside the Group's purpose or remit. In particular, it is important that the terms of reference of the Group are well understood and agreed in order that expectations of members are in line with the way the nursery intends to act on the discussion held. Steering groups are an essential component of workplace nursery status, under HM Revenue and Customs* rules, and it is important that the group considers policy issues, and that the employer sponsor is centrally involved. However a steering group can also offer a good way of informing the nursery about local initiatives and schools that children may well transfer to, if community representatives are also invited to attend.

All these different ways of communicating with parents, and encourage-ments to working as partners in the care and education of their young children, help us to reassure parents of the benefits of using a nursery, and remind them of our policies on the difficult issues of managing children's behaviour and dealing with childhood illnesses. They also help us to keep in touch with parents' changing needs and aspirations.

NETWORKING

A nursery can benefit a great deal from being part of the community it serves. This sounds obvious, but it is frequently not the case because of the way in which it came into being or because of where it is located. If the nursery is to benefit, its relationship with the community needs to go further than the formal liaison with other professionals required under the Children Act provisions which protect the welfare and health of the child.

The new focus on collaboration across public, private and voluntary sectors, enshrined in *Every Child Matters**, implies that all nurseries should be more concerned with outreach into the community so that all families know about, and have a chance to access their facilities through creative ways of joining in activities. A nursery should reflect the diversity of the local population, respect local cultures and seek feedback to ensure the nursery's service responds to their needs. By working in this way, those providers who have been entirely independent in the past will be able to identify opportunities to participate in the Labour Government's vision of Children's Centres in every community, which are now in the hands of local authorities to commission.

Community links

As part of the nursery curriculum children will visit local libraries, swimming pools, parks, and other resources that add richness to daily activities. They also have the opportunity to do things they would be doing if they were with their parents, such as shopping and going for walks. Ideally the nursery children will visit schools and be invited to watch special shows and assemblies to introduce them to school life. All this activity can help to broaden the children's perspective and encourage them to explore places and people in a positive way.

However, this can be a two-way process, with the nursery offering some of its resources to others in the community. Schoolchildren can be invited to observe some of the nursery routines; and nursery dancing and music classes can be extended to children in the care of local childminders – also providing an opportunity for the carers to get to know the nursery staff. Holiday playschemes based in the nursery can be offered to children who have gone to school before the age of five.

APPENDIX TO CHAPTER 5

TERMS AND CONDITIONS OF BUSINESS

The following are the terms and conditions of business of ('the Company'). By signing the application form and applying for a place at one of the Company's nurseries ('the Nursery') you agree to be bound by these terms, which can only be varied if such variation is agreed in writing and signed by an authorised representative of the Company.

1 Deposit

A deposit is payable and returnable to the Company with the application form. The deposit is held by the Company with the application until your child leaves the Nursery when (provided written notice of withdrawal has been given to the Company in accordance with paragraph 4 below and all fees and other charges are paid up to date) it will be refunded to you. Interest does not accrue on the deposit.

2 Acceptance

The Company will send a written acceptance of your application for a place at the Nursery. Deposits paid with applications that cannot be accepted will be refunded immediately.

3 Fees

3.1 Fees for each calendar month are payable in advance by direct debit on the 25th day of the previous calendar month.

3.2 Fees due for periods of part of a month at the beginning of your child's attendance at the Nursery are payable one month before your child's starting date and will be invoiced separately.

3.3 Fees due for periods of part of a month at the end of your child's attendance at the Nursery are payable by cheque on the 25th day of the month preceding your child's departure and will be invoiced separately.

3.4 Payment for extra hours for pre-school children and extra days for babies, toddlers and pre-school children which are needed on an ad hoc basis will be invoiced separately and are payable by cheque on or in advance of the date the extra noun or days are required.

3.5 Fees are payable throughout the period that your child is due to attend the Nursery and no rebate will be made for absence due to sickness, family holidays or any other reasons.

3.6 No refund of fees will be made if you postpone the date your child starts at the Nursery to a date later than the agreed starting date.

3.7 The Company reserves the right not to admit your child to the Nursery in the event of non-payment of fees or cancellation of your direct debit.

3.8 Fees are subject to review and can be increased at the Company's discretion without notice and at any time.

4 **Notice of withdrawal/change in requirements**

4.1 From the time the Company accepts your application for a place at the Nursery in accordance with paragraph 2 above three months written notice must be given to the Company (time to be of the essence) in order to:-

4.1.1 withdraw your child from the Nursery;

4.1.2 delay or cancel your child's starting dare at the Nursery;

4.1.3 decrease the number of hours in a day or days in a week that your child attends the Nursery.

4.2 Failure to give the required written notice in accordance with 4.1.1 and 4.1.2 above will result in fees being payable for the appropriate period in lieu of the full notice that should have been given.

4.3 Failure to give the reqired written notice in accordance with Clause 4.1.3 above will result in fees being payable for the original hours and/or days until the three months notice period would have expired if properly given.

4.4 Notice of withdrawal or change in requirements is deemed to commence on the date that the written notice is received by the Company.

4.5 If you wish to cancel your child's place at the Nursery following the Company's written acceptance in accordance with paragraph 2 but prior to your child starting at the Nursery and 3 months' notice is served by you to this effect in accordance with paragraph 4.1, the deposit paid with the acceptance form will be returned to you subject to an administration charge of £50.00.

5 **Recovery of unpaid fees**

The Company reserves the right to charge interest at the rate of 2 per cent per month on all outstanding fees. You will also be responsible for the payment of all additional charges incurred by the Company in the collection of outstanding fees including but not limited to our internal administrative charges and our solicitors' costs and disbursements.

6 **Child's details**

6.1 The Nursery requires and will rely on derailed information relating to your child as contained in the Company's consent and information form which shall form part of this contract. The Company must be immediately informed in writing of any changes to the information provided and is not liable for the consequences of your failure to update the information.

6.2 The Company will require you to fully complete and sign the consent and information form prior to leaving your child at the Nursery.

7 **Removal of child**

The Company reserves the right to require the removal of a child from the Nursery on a temporary or permanent basis at its discretion. In the event of permanent removal fees will be payable for the then current month but no further payments will be due in lieu of notice. No refund of fees will be made for temporary removal.

8 **Generally**

8.1 No failure or delay on behalf of the Company to exercise any right or remedy under these terms and conditions shall be construed or operate as a waiver.

8.2 This contract including all disputes hereunder shall be interpreted and resolved in accordance with the laws of England.

Chapter 6

Working to a plan

- Running a nursery is running a small business
- Business planning
- Setting objectives
- Understanding the language of finance
- Performance measurement
- Sources of finance
- Setting fees
- Risk assessment

RUNNING A NURSERY IS RUNNING A SMALL BUSINESS

Parents in the UK spent an estimated £2.6 billion on nursery services in 2005, paying average full-time fees of £135.50 per week, which equates to approximately 77 per cent of the actual cost of the service. Employers funded 12.5 per cent of costs through workplace nurseries and *Childcare Vouchers** (£420 million). Direct government subsidy through the Nursery Education Grant* for three and four year olds amounted to £260 million, and indirect subsidies through *Working Families Tax Credit** have been valued at £325 million. The balance would appear to be in the widening tax reliefs, suggesting that the total government contribution amounts to just over 20 per cent (Laing and Buisson, March 2006).

An estimated total of 255 nursery groups (with more than three nurseries) account for 17.5 per cent of total UK childcare places (Laing and Buisson, March 2006), and the number of larger groups grew by a third in the previous four years. The market is still highly fragmented, with many companies seeking to expand, despite the lowest fee increases on record in 2005, falling occupancies and increasing staff costs. Acquisition and merger activity has never been greater, both between groups and from venture capitalists and other care service companies, and several childcare companies are now quoted on the stock market. Supply of child-care places has outstripped demand in the private sector for several years, exacerbated by new competition from Sure Start and Children's Centres, and schools providing nursery classes.

Nurseries are small businesses, whether they are a single operation, part of a larger group, contained within a school or one service offered by a Children's Centre. They are all subject to the same financial pressures and the same external issues such as staff salary costs and increasing demands of the registration and inspection system. But because we all serve children and families, who rely on us to provide their children with a good start so that they can pursue work or other priorities in their lives, we have the added imperative of ensuring that our businesses are sustainable. It is different from a supermarket withdrawing a product and customers having to choose something else or having to wait a further week to get the car serviced. While we have the interests of children and families at the heart of what we do, we need to be reliable and permanent.

The continuous challenge for a nursery service is the balance of cost and quality: to provide a service that meets regulatory expectations is to provide the minimum that earns a licence to operate at all. To provide a service that keeps up with parents' expectations and needs, particularly in relation to increasingly flexible work patterns, is more costly; to provide a service that anticipates and prepares for the next level of understanding of child development, or human resources practice, or community outreach, remains for many an aspiration. However, because we know about the research that provides us with deeper insights into better practice and improved outcomes for children and families, how can we hold back from incorporating it into our service? The risk we run is that the costs of our service will then become unaffordable for many parents, given that they will be funding, broadly, 77 per cent themselves.

One of the pressing concerns is to find the money for training and development, given that the undertaking of such activities also takes staff out of the nursery, and they need cover in order to maintain ratios. Such costs can be budgeted at the outset, correspondingly increasing fees, or they can be funded from surplus funds, which, of course, may not transpire. This example serves to illustrate how small the difference is between the various sectors of public, voluntary and private childcare. The former two sectors are more likely to budget up front, and the latter is more likely to afford training and development if it can. The former two may end up with a deficit, but the latter will not – because it cannot, as it is a for-profit business with directors who have a fiduciary duty to make sure the business continues to be viable. Which is serving children and families best?

Looking at this issue from a working parent's perspective, there is another dimension, and that is the availability of appropriate childcare – childcare that matches their work pattern. If a childcare provision is both available and of the right quality, then it is probably unaffordable; if it is both available and affordable, it is probably not of sufficient quality or appropriate to their needs; if it is affordable and of the right quality, it is probably very full, with a long waiting list, and therefore unavailable.

Bright Horizons Family Solutions has illustrated this 'Trilemma' for the purpose of encouraging employers to understand the difference their contribution can make – see Figure 6.1.

Nursery managers may not be responsible for such strategic moves, but they need to be aware that these are the kinds of pressure the business will be responding to – and that means finding ways in which the nursery can incorporate the thinking.

Nursery managers will always be action-oriented, practical organisers. These are key requirements for the post. However, the application of

The Childcare Trilemma

Quality care is expensive

- Entails more labour-intensive ratios and smaller group sizes
- Requires educated, trained workforce
- Exceeds minimum registration standards of health, safety and education

Economics of care creates shortages

- Reflects high-cost/low-return business reality
- Severe lack of infant/toddler care due to higher ratios
- Days and hours of care are limited and may not match employee's needs

ACCESSIBILITY

Access to quality care is limited

- Government initiatives have increased demand, not supply
- Care hours are not flexible to meet the needs of working parents
- High quality care emphasising education is harder to find than custodial care, which is not focused on enriching the child

FIGURE 6.1 The Childcare Trilemma

these skills can be transformed if they can be related to the key objectives of the business, which may be the nursery itself, or it may be a broader organisation. This means understanding the *business plan*. A business plan may comprise a set of statements and columns of figures on one side of A4, or it may be a weighty reference document that is brought out of the drawer, dusted off, and reviewed by committee every few years. Whatever the format, the business plan places today's activities in the context of where the business is heading. If your nursery does not have one, it would be worthwhile to construct one. At the very least, it will help with responsibilities at management level. It will also help to ensure that activities have a purpose, and that one purpose is consistent with another.

BUSINESS PLANNING

The preparation of a business plan should not be a once-and-for-all exercise. The process of examining what you want to do and testing its viability is as important as the successful outcome and achievement of the plan itself.

149

As with any plan, a business plan enables you to drive your business forward, rather than being left to respond to the myriad of internal and external factors affecting everyday business life. It is this self-focus and analysis which lies at the heart of the process and is its most valuable and lasting aspect. However, a more usual imperative for the preparation of a business plan is the need to supply a bank with sufficient information on which to make a decision to lend you money. A third, and frequently overlooked, reason for preparing a business plan is to make clear to staff what is before the organisation – where it is aiming to be in the months and years ahead.

The most valuable use of my own business plan has been to provide me with a means of anticipating the effects of change. Reference points are important as a marker, against which new ideas can be measured. A business plan lays down such markers, and provides a basis on which to consider how changes will affect the business. In a way, a business plan is a series of layers of information. If a change requires you to adjust the top layer, it is probably something that can be incorporated into day-to-day activity quite easily. If, however, the change demands a reassessment at the deepest level, then the process of addressing the change may be painful, and touch on fundamental values.

A business plan should have three broad sections:

- A section on your service and the marketplace will cover what your service consists of and how it is distinctive. It will identify who your clients will be and why they need and are likely to buy the services you are to provide. The general marketing environment will be covered – is it a growth area, and who are your competitors? What will selling your service depend on – what are your critical success factors? This first section amounts to the *marketing plan.*

- The second part will focus on *how* the service will be delivered. An analysis of your own strengths and weaknesses will help to identify what other skills and experiences you will need to buy in and where you are likely to find them. Having decided on what your service consists of, you are in a position to calculate how many staff you will need to employ and the profile of the staff team. Assessing the capability of the whole staff team will lead to the need for computers, systems and procedures, and other *non-human* resources. You will then have your *resources plan.*

150

- Finally, you need to quantify what the marketing and resources plans imply in terms of funding, and what they will deliver in terms of revenue. The most critical aspect of this part of the business plan is to lay out your *planning assumptions* – i.e. the basis on which you are going to collect and use income in the delivery of your service. How profitable will the operation be, and what will be the cash requirements of the organisation? And what if some of your planning assumptions are wrong? Just how wrong can you afford to be, and for how long, and what action can be taken to put it right?

Before going on to discuss a business plan in more detail, it is worth saying that the plan should be appropriate for the size of your business – it does not need to be a small volume! Its essential purpose is to demonstrate that you have thought through the issues of running your nursery as a business, that you have thought about the threats to stability it might face, and that the figures involved look sensible.

At this point many management books quote the experience of Anita Roddick, who was turned down flat by a bank on production of her first business plan, when asking for a £4,000 loan to start up Bodyshop. The rest is part of business planning folklore!

SETTING OBJECTIVES

At the beginning of every business planning cycle – i.e. when you set out and when you review the way in which you wish to move forward – you need to look at your prime objectives. If you cannot identify these, then that too tells you something.

Nursery nurses are used to planning. What is more, they are used to making plans on the basis of observation of the requirements of children. It is this same approach that the business plan needs. Why are you really doing this? What is your *mission* in running a nursery? This is the start of the planning process:

- a statement of mission;
- a statement of objectives;
- identification of tasks;
- formulation of action plans.

Note that mission statements and objectives are 'what' statements, whereas tasks and action plans are 'how to' statements – what to do on Monday morning.

Mission statements and objectives are *directional,* intended to focus your attention on the essentials that encapsulate your special *competencies* to deliver the service to the parents and children you intend to satisfy. It is through being very specific that a small business can differentiate itself from its larger competitors. This is often described as a *personal service* – a service that has not lost its distinctive character through becoming larger and sometimes less focused.

The mission statement

The mission statement should explain what business you are in and include some or all of the following:

- For *what* reason are you are doing this?
- *Who* are you trying to satisfy?
- With *what* services will you meet that demand?
- *How* will you deliver the services?
- *Where* will you be in the future?

Above all, mission statements should be realistic, achievable and brief. My own, prepared in 1992, is shown in Figure 6.2.

MISSION STATEMENT

- Our mission is to be the leading nursery provider in the UK, offering a premium service to working parents that is distinctive for its unique qualities and professional integrity.

- Our main purpose will be supported by the further developments of our innovative childcare strategy consultancy service in order that we remain at the forefront of the industry,

- Our business strategy is based on our commitment to people development. We see this as our most effective route to maintain our industry leader position.

FIGURE 6.2 A mission statement

Andrew Campbell, director of the London-based Ashbridge Strategic Management Centre, has said:

> Many of the world's outstanding companies employ people with what we call 'a sense of mission'. They believe that their company is special and they are proud to be a part of it.

Campbell headed a research project into how managers can better understand and create a sense of mission in their organisations. He is convinced that firms increasingly need passionate employees, and says:

> Many organisations have become depersonalised to the point where energy levels are low, cynicism is high and work fails to excite or fulfil employees. We find that committed staff perform many times more effectively . . .

I think that, generally, such sentiments do not characterise a nursery team. In my experience, nursery staff feel passionately about what they do and have an exceptionally strong sense of commitment towards children and parents. But do they feel the same about nursery organisation? If the answer to this is No, then it is probably because the organisation has not shared its mission.

After a study of more than 100 statements from American, Japanese and European companies, the Ashbridge Centre concluded that these statements in themselves had little impact on business success. Much more important was whether a sense of mission already existed in the hearts and minds of employees. Employees not only need to have a clear understanding of what their company is trying to achieve, but also need to be emotionally committed to its aims before a meaningful statement can be written. If commitment is lacking, a mission statement is at best likely to be ignored and at worst treated with cynicism. From these findings, Campbell set out five principles to help managers trying to create a sense of mission (see Figure 6.3).

'Leaders should not forget that although a sense of mission is an emotional force it can be managed,' Campbell says. 'It is an aspect of business which cannot be ignored. An organisation with a sense of mission has a strong advantage.'

1	Leaders should pick a theme around which to develop a mission. It should capture the business' future strategy and values, and should be easy to translate into behaviour and standards.
2	Focus on action rather than words.
3	Standards and behaviour should clearly affirm the business' new direction.
4	Be patient – developing a mission takes years.
5	Build and sustain trust. This is often achieved by senior management being visible and open about changes taking place.

FIGURE 6.3 Principles on which to create a sense of mission

The objectives

Setting your objectives is about how you intend to fulfil your mission. It is your *success strategy* – how you will survive and thrive *and* remain true to your mission.

Most commonly, small businesses set their objectives in revenue terms: what do we want or need our income to be, and by when? However, for nurseries, the focus of attention is *occupancy* rather than *turnover,* as a measurement of business success.

You will need to set objectives under the following headings, and for the short term (18 months) and longer term:

- *Size:* How big do you want to be and by when?
- *Reputation:* What do you want people to think of your nursery?
- *Profitability:* What do you want to earn from it?
- *Future:* What are your longer term aspirations?

Your objectives may be very personal, particularly if you own the business (e.g. 'I want to ensure that in 5 years' time the nursery is profitable enough to be sold and to allow me to retire'). Or they may be less to do with you and more to do with growth of the business (e.g. 'I want to build our reputation for offering value for money services to working parents'), hence safeguarding your ability to take on workplace nursery contracts.

For your objectives to work they need to meet eight criteria:

- *They must be measurable.* You can get the business to where you want it to be only by setting specific targets. These need not always be financial, but may relate to a low staff turnover, or a percentage of the occupancy coming from the local residential community.

- *They should be realistic but challenging.* The objectives need to stretch everyone a little further than they want to go, but within the boundaries of possibility. For example, if your goal is to pay nursery staff the best salaries, but your nursery fees are at the bottom of the league, it is unlikely that anyone will believe in your objectives.

- *They should have timescales.* Every objective should have a date set for its achievement. Becoming profitable 'as soon as possible' requires a very different approach from becoming profitable 'within 18 months'.

- *They require consultation.* People responsible for achieving objectives need to be involved in setting them, and they must understand that they are responsible for achieving them. As the nursery manager, you have the responsibility of indicating what you believe to be appropriate objectives, but you need to carry others with you.

- *They must be communicated.* Every team member needs to know where the nursery is headed and what they stand to gain if this is achieved. This is not necessarily money, but could be career development, broadened responsibility, or improved terms of employment.

- *They should be capable of monitoring against performance.* If not, people will think that you don't really care whether they are achieved or not.

- *They should be capable of being challenged.* Team members need to feel that they can challenge your objectives. You may like to invite them to prepare their own, and to compare achievability with yours.

- *They need to be updated.* Objectives are based on assumptions about the internal and external worlds of the nursery. The market you intended to serve may change: a local factory closes; a school suddenly opens its own nursery class; or revised registration requirements suggest a totally new staffing framework, involving you in additional costs.

Figure 6.4 gives a general indication of how small companies go about setting objectives. The results show that internal criteria are more of a driving force than market-led criteria.

MEETING YOUR OBJECTIVES

Comparison with key competitors	41%
Comparison with business sector overall	49%
Self-determined standards	66%
Company strategy	68%
Comparison with own previous performance	76%

Source: Peat Marwick (1990)

FIGURE 6.4 What are the objectives based on?

Meeting your objectives

Although making detailed comparisons with the competition is unlikely to be something you find terribly useful or central to what you do, you need to understand that parents will be doing just that.

We positively encourage parents to look around before making a final selection. This enables them to understand for themselves how our service differs and why our fees are what they are! Having looked at a number of others, if parents then make a positive choice in favour of our nursery, they are unlikely to waiver at a later date.

However, you can provide parents with information that helps them to see the differences between your nursery and others. Parents need to know how your service will benefit them and their child. They tend to be less interested in your perspective on child development or the academic underpinning for the nursery's philosophy. What we may feel proud of as elements of our service need to give way to the promises and guarantees we are prepared to offer parents.

Once you have established what you are offering, and to whom, you can make the *features* of your service be seen in terms of the *benefits* parents get when they book a place for their child. Features are what a service has or is; benefits are what the features mean for the parent and child.

The financial plan

The financial plan seeks to reflect the implications of your marketing and operational plans, in the form of profit-and-loss accounts, cash flows and balance sheets. Different strategies or variations of existing ones are tested to validate their effect on the project's financial performance.

The believability of any business plan will depend greatly on the assumptions that underpin it. These assumptions should cover the key areas of business and its operating environment. You also need to assess the downside risk and show how far things can go before new action has to be taken. Your assumptions can be recorded and monitored using a table like that in Figure 6.5.

UNDERSTANDING THE LANGUAGE OF FINANCE

Liquidators – who ought to know why businesses fail if anyone does – put 'lack of reliable financial information' at the top of their list. Many failed entrepreneurs believe accounting to be a bureaucratic nuisance carried out for the benefit of the Inland Revenue alone. These same people, who would never drive a car without a fuel gauge, speedometer, or oil pressure indicator, frequently set off at breakneck speed running their business only with a 'gut feeling' or perhaps the annual accounts to guide them. For them the end of the first year is often the end of the business.

Taking the analogy further, the motorist must also plan ahead to arrive successfully at the desired destination safely and on time. The success of any journey – particularly a long one – depends very much on the care taken at this stage. The preparation must centre around three distinct areas:

- the car: making sure it is serviced, filled with fuel and generally in a fit state to make the journey;
- the route: choosing one that takes account of other traffic, possible roadworks, and facilities en route such as petrol, refreshments, etc.;

Key assumptions	Basis of assumption	Confidence in assumption	What would happen if this assumption proved incorrect?
1			
2			
3			
4			
5			

FIGURE 6.5 A table like this can be used to identify how robust your assumptions are

- the travellers: ensuring that everyone is prepared for the journey.

If this stage is accomplished with reasonable care and attention, the travellers and their vehicle have a very good chance of success in the next phase, which is the journey itself.

The most sound approach to the journey is to assess the distance to be travelled, determine an average travelling speed that is maintainable and safe, and from this determine the time needed to travel the distance. Then, working back from when you want to arrive, and allowing a margin of safety for petrol stops, refreshments, etc., you can calculate when you must set off. The rest of the journey should be plain sailing provided you follow your plan, follow the map correctly, and take account of the warning signs along the route. In all probability you will arrive at your destination safely and on time.

There are many parallels between planning a car journey and planning a business.

The balance sheet

You need a method of periodically measuring the growth and development of your venture. The balance sheet is a 'snapshot' which shows where the money came from to fund the business and where it was spent – at a fixed point in time, usually at annual intervals. The *'where it came from'* will usually include your own cash, share capital, the profit generated to date and loans received to date (both long-term and short-term). The *'where it went to'* will usually include fixed assets, stocks, debtors, plus the cash left in the *'tank'*. The comparison with motoring would be the milometer which measures the absolute distance the car has travelled, as opposed to the relative or changing performance measurement offered by the speedometer.

Profit-and-loss account

This is another moving picture of how well the business is doing, in terms of costs and profitability – usually prepared on a monthly basis but covering an accounting period of one year. This can be compared to the speedometer in the car which constantly changes as the car progresses on its journey. The profit-and-loss account monitors the day-to-day performance of the business and gives the business person the information needed to identify the areas where corrective action should be taken – the equivalent of slowing down and taking notice of the road signs.

The business plan forecasts what these statements will look like at various points in the future. It is your first *operating budget*.

Operating budgets

A lot of businesses do not make a profit or have enough cash at the right time because the management has not planned ahead. Too often, they do not know how much profit or loss has been made until months after the end of the financial year. And often, profit is not properly thought out until there is a crisis.

Budgeting gives you a useful planning tool. By comparing your actual performance with the budget, you can spot difficulties early on and take action to put them right. However, all budgets are based on assumptions, so these must be specific and as realistic as possible.

In your operating budgets you can build-in contingencies to cover unexpected expenditure. A contingency can be shown as a separate item or included in the individual cost figures.

Costs

You must also be clear about the difference between the various costs of running your business. Some will vary depending on how well your business is doing. Some will not change.

Variable costs

Also known as 'direct costs', your variable costs are linked directly to producing your service. They are the costs of your new materials, and so on, as well as the wages of your employees who actually produce the service, i.e. not administrative staff.

Fixed costs

You will have to meet these costs, even if you do not sell places. They include rent, rates, heating, lighting, insurance and fixed salaries, including your own. They are also known as 'indirect costs' or 'overheads'.

Depreciation

Depreciation takes into account the reduction in value of an asset over its working life. It is thus an expense, and so you should charge it to the profit-and-loss account, and include it in the operating budget.

Cash flow

This is a moving picture of how well the business is doing, in terms of cash movements. It bears a very close resemblance to the profit-and-loss account but reflects the effect the *credit taken from suppliers* and *given to parents* has on the cash in the business.

Profit does not always equal cash. Here the comparison with the car is particularly apt. A car needs petrol to run and the petrol gauge shows how much there is in the tank; a business needs cash to survive and the cash-flow statement shows how much there is in the business 'tank'.

Cash-flow forecasting

Once you have worked out an operating budget, you are ready to move on to produce a cash-flow forecast.

Unlike your operating budget, your cash-flow forecast is not to do with profit and loss. It is just your best estimate of how the cash will go in and out of your bank account over a certain period.

Cash is the lifeblood of your business. Managing cash badly is one of the main reasons for business failure. The time you spend working out your cash needs and monitoring cash flow is time well spent. This is because you can:

- find out when you might not have enough cash before it happens;
- find out when you might make extra cash and use it efficiently;
- make sure you have enough cash for any necessary capital expenditure;
- find out how to use your resources more efficiently and reduce costs.

Like your operating budget, your cash-flow forecast will be based upon assumptions. Again you must be realistic. Think about the best and worst cases and explain the assumptions you make. The more realistic your forecasts, the better any bank will like them:

- Think about the period of credit you will give to your parents or take from your suppliers. For example, suppose you can keep your parents to 30 days' credit (which will not be easy). Your *operating budget* could show the fees you invoiced, say, in January, but this cash should not be in your cash-flow projection until February – and then only if you are sure your parents will pay on time. If you have never had dealings with your suppliers before, you might have to settle their bills immediately. Obviously this will affect your cash flow – you will be buying things before your client pays for them.

- Your forecast should show all cash you will pay and receive, including your own salary, capital spending and loans. These are all part of your cash flow. However, depreciation is not, because it is only a notional book entry – it does not mean real cash coming in or going out of the business.

Break-even analysis

With the information contained in the above financial statements, the manager will know whether the business has made a profit or loss in the past, but may not know whether it is still making a profit. A break-even analysis will show the level of sales required to generate sufficient profit to cover the overheads of the business, and thereby break even. The manager can then be confident that if he or she trades at above this break-even level of sales, the business will be operating profitably, barring any changes in the level of profit and overheads.

In car terms, the driver knows that in order to arrive at her destination on time she has to average so many miles per hour, say 50. If the driver averages less than 50 miles per hour, then she will be late; conversely if the driver exceeds it for any length of time she will arrive early. The 50 miles per hour is her break-even point. In business terms arriving early equals making a profit, and arriving late equals making a loss.

You need a clear appreciation from the outset that profit is not cash, and cash is not profit. In the short term, a small business can survive even if it is not making a profit, provided it has sufficient cash reserves, but it cannot survive for long without cash even though it may be making a profit. The purpose of the cash-flow projection is to calculate how much cash a business is likely to need to accomplish its objectives, and when it will need it. The projections will form the basis of negotiations with any potential provider of capital.

PERFORMANCE MEASUREMENT

The most important reason for having plans becomes clear when you begin to evaluate performance against them. To know that you are on track, where you and others expect you to be, is tantamount to your success as a manager. A recognised way of assessing financial performance is by the use of *key ratios*.

A ratio is something expressed as a proportion of something else. For example, a percentage is a ratio, where something is compared with a base of 100.

Key ratios point to questions about the business that need answers. They allow a manager to choose, from the hundreds of questions that might be asked, the handful that are really worth answering. In a small business, time is at a premium. This quick pre-selection is essential.

What are the key ratios?

Bear in mind that *profitability* is sales income or value of services sold, *minus* the cost of sales (i.e. everything that has gone into delivering that service – these are the direct or variable costs), i.e. the costs that are incurred entirely because of the service being supplied. For example, rent would be incurred whatever the business was supplying; staff in ratio to children would be employed only for a nursery service.

Gross profit ratio

Deduct the cost of sales from sales, and express the result as a proportion of sales by dividing by sales.

Operating profit ratio

Deduct overheads from the gross profit, and divide by sales. Overheads are your indirect or fixed costs.

This ratio demonstrates the importance of profit, whereas increased sales are not meaningful in themselves. If the ratio is too low, the manager should perhaps be looking for savings in administration, or ensuring that marketing effort is more closely targeted to result in higher occupancy.

Liquidity ratio

This ratio checks your cash position, whether you have enough working capital and whether you can meet your debts as they fall due.

'Debtors + cash' divided by 'creditors' should be 1:1. A lower ratio is risky A higher ratio indicates that too much money is owed to you or that your borrowing is too high. Either way you are taking an unnecessary level of financial risk, and suppliers may stop supplying or even petition for bankruptcy.

Because the cash position is critical in a small business, creditor and debtor policies are very important.

How many times can you cover current liabilities? 'Debtors + cash' divided by 'bills and interest due' should be 1:1. A lower ratio is risky. A much higher ratio indicates that too much money is owed to you or that your borrowing is too high.

SOURCES OF FINANCE

Two sources of funds are most commonly used:

* lenders;
* investors, including yourself.

Anyone lending money to, or investing in, a venture will expect the entrepreneur to have given some thought to the lender's or investor's needs, and to have explained how they can be accommodated in the business plan.

Banks, and indeed any other sources of debt capital, look for asset security to back their loans, and the near certainty of getting their money back. They charge an interest rate that reflects current market conditions and their view of the risk level of the proposal. Depending on the nature of the business in question and the purpose for which the money is being used, banks will take a five- to fifteen-year view.

As with a house mortgage repayment, banks will usually expect a business to start repaying both the loan and the interest on a monthly or quarterly basis immediately the loan has been granted. In some cases a capital 'holiday' for up to two years can be negotiated, but in the early stage of any loan the interest charge makes up the lion's share of repayments.

The lending bank will hope that the business will be a success so that it can lend more money in the future and provide more banking services such as insurance, tax advice, etc. to a loyal customer. The bank will be less interested in rapid growth and the consequent capital gain than in a steady stream of earnings almost from the outset.

As most new or fast-growing businesses generally do not make immediate profits, money for such enterprises must come from elsewhere. Risk or equity capital, as other types of funds are called, comes from venture capital houses (as well as being put in by founders, their families and friends). Because the inherent risks involved in investing in new and young ventures are greater than for investing in established companies, venture capital fund managers have to offer their investors the chance of larger overall returns. To do that, fund managers must not only keep failures to a minimum, they have to pick some big winners too – ventures with annual compound growth rates above 50 per cent – to offset the inevitable mediocre performers.

Typically, from any ten investments a fund manager would expect one star, seven also-rans, and two flops. However, it is important to remember that, despite this outcome, venture capital fund managers are looking only for winners, so unless you are projecting high capital growth, the chances of getting venture capital are against you.

Not only do venture capitalists look for winners, they also look for a substantial shareholding in your business. There are no simple rules for what constitutes a fair split, but *Venture Capital Report,* a UK monthly publication of investment opportunities, suggests the following starting point:

For the idea	33 per cent
For the management	33 per cent
For the money	34 per cent

It all comes down to how badly you need the money, how risky the venture is, how much money could be made – and your skills as a negotiator. However, it is salutary to remember that 100 per cent of nothing is still nothing, so all parties to the deal have to be satisfied if it is to succeed.

A venture capital firm may also want to put a non-executive director on the board of your company to look after its interests. You will then have at your disposal a talented financial brain, so be prepared to make use of him or her. This service will not be free – you will either pay 'up front' in the fee for raising the capital, or you will pay an annual management charge.

As a fast-growing company typically has no cash available to pay dividends, investors can profit only by selling their shareholdings. With this in mind the venture capitalist needs to have an exit route in view at the outset, such as the Stock Exchange or a potential corporate buyer. Unlike many entrepreneurs (and some lending banks) who see their ventures as life-long commitments to success and growth, venture capitalists have a relatively short time horizon. Typically they aim to liquidate small company investments within three to seven years, allowing them to pay out individual investors and to have funds available for tomorrow's winners.

So, to be successful your business finances must take account of the needs of these two types of sources of finance. The factors are summarised in Figure 6.6.

Getting a grant

Another source of money is neither debt nor equity, and in theory is free. The magic money source is called a 'grant'. The EU, the UK government and many local authorities give grants for one purpose or another. Various

Lenders (any safe bet)	Investors (winners only)
• Security and low risk	• High risk but high returns
• 5-15-year horizon	• 3–7-year horizon
• Ability to pay back loan and interest immediately	• 35% compound growth minimum, but no payments until the end of the deal
• conservative growth	• Large sums, with few top-ups
• Small sums, with frequent top-ups	• Substantial shareholding:
• No share of future profits, but want a loyal long-term customer	– for the idea 33%
• No management involvement	– for management 33%
	– for money 34%
	• Exit route evident at outset:
	– back to founders
	– trade buyer
	– USM etc.
	• Hands-on involvement

FIGURE 6.6 Factors to bear in mind with lenders and investors

estimates put the total figure of grant aid available at between £500 million and £2 billion a year. *Sources of Grant Aid for Business in the UK* is a 2,000-page, looseleaf and regularly updated guide to grants, published by Weka Publishing Ltd, 74–80 Camden Street, London NW1 1YW.

Before you rush off and search for this 'free money', do remember that someone giving a grant often wants you to do something that does not make commercial sense. Over the past ten years many funding streams have been made available to set up or expand nurseries, to increase the quantity of childcare, particularly in disadvantaged areas. The business needs to be sure that its objectives will be furthered, not compromised, by the conditions attached to the grant.

The golden rule is: Decide what you want to do and check that it makes sound business sense; then see if anyone will fund you to do it.

SETTING FEES

When considering what fee levels should be, the most frequent mistake is to set them too low. This can occur either through failing to understand all the costs associated with planning and delivering the service, or through yielding to the temptation to under-cut or certainly not exceed fees charged by other nurseries. Both are usually fatal.

The nursery manager is the very best source of information on fees. The manager sees parents, hears their response to fees as quoted, and hears them compare the fees with those of other nurseries visited and other forms of childcare. It is useful to devise a form for feedback for those parents who visit but do not take up a place at the nursery, as it is equally very easy to blame price, when actually the reasons may be more complex.

There are internal and external issues that need to be considered when setting fees.

Internal issues

Costs

Make sure you have identified *all* the costs you are likely to incur in planning and delivering your service. Surprisingly this is often forgotten. If staff are going to have non-contact time for observation and activity planning, cover will need to be supplied if the nursery is to remain open. If there are to be 'inset' training days, then there is a cost to be covered, although fees may not be chargeable because the nursery will be closed.

Quality of service

The positioning of the service in the market is influenced largely by the fees/quality relationship. This is shown in Figure 6.7.

A confident approach would be to position the nursery in (4), (7) or (8) because they offer high value for money. Strategies (2), (3) and (6) may suit the short term but are unlikely to be sustainable over time.

Policy

The overall image you want to portray will also influence the fees you wish to charge. Running a nursery is not typical in business terms. Registration under the Children Act requires a certain level of costs to be incurred and a certain quality of service to be delivered. There are no serious and sustainable, cheap and cheerful nursery businesses. If parents regard the Children Act levels as par, then anything over and above the cheapest service they have come across needs to justify its higher prices. It is also a business in which 'gloss' in any form is seen to detract from the real benefits to children.

Where nurseries maintain fees at levels that barely cover costs, a number of people have undoubtedly been discouraged from starting new nurseries. In areas where nurseries have charged higher fees, new competitors have been attracted into the market.

Capacity

Capacity to provide childcare places will also influence fees charged. How fast the nursery will fill is a key factor in whether the nursery is viable and should not be underestimated in its importance. It is also important to remember that, once full, no more places can be sold. This is another

	Low fees	Medium fees	High fees
Low quality	Cheap value (1)	Out of step (2)	Exploitive (3)
Medium quality	Above-average value (4)	Middle of road (5)	Overcharging (6)
High quality	Superb value (7)	High value (8)	Premium (9)

 **FIGURE 6.7** The fees/quality approach

factor that distinguishes the nursery business from many other small-business operations. Fees must be set at a level that will work, or can be reached, when the nursery is full, as well as when it is starting out. What will your fees need to be to cover your (high proportion of) fixed costs at the outset? Will this be higher than it needs to be when you are at 50 per cent/85 per cent full, and how will you handle that? Will you operate at a loss to begin with, or will you plan to make a proportionately higher return as the nursery fills?

External issues

Parents' perceptions

Because childcare has grown up in this country through the strong traditions of the public and voluntary sectors, it is only relatively recently that the true costs of providing nursery services have become general knowledge. Parents' opinion of value may still bear little or no relation to the cost, and because there are still many areas of the country that have little or no provision they may have little knowledge of competitive charges.

Fees convey a message to parents – that the service is 'budget', 'middle of the road' or 'top drawer'. Parents use fees to confirm their impression of the service and thereby make a choice. In this way, when you set a fee, you select the market of parents you wish to target. The three terms used above are difficult to use in relation to nursery services. 'Top drawer', as indicated by fees charged, in the view of many commentators would simply imply a service to which all children are entitled and which discerning parents should expect.

Competition

It is usually a misconception to think that new nurseries can undercut fees charged by established competitors. This is probably based on a misunderstanding of the real overheads and a lack of appreciation that 'unit' costs fall in proportion to experience – i.e. the time needed to undertake a task when you are experienced at it and have developed a system, in contrast to the first attempts.

Clearly it is important to take account of what competitors charge, because this provides an indication of what parents expect to pay. But fees are the easiest element of business to vary. The competition could follow you down the fees curve, forcing you into failure, far more easily than you could capture their parents with lower fees.

Business conditions

The overall conditions in the marketplace will have a bearing on setting fees, although it is not an industry in which parents 'shop around' for keener prices alone. In times of recession parents will (and did) question fees more than at other times; but because so high a proportion of costs – and therefore fees – is devoted to staff costs, parents can usually discern from the impression they get from staff, and the service they observe, whether the fee matches the service. If there are more staff around, and the nursery appears calm and uncluttered, and the children are engaged in activities, most parents will appreciate that there will be a correspondingly high fee level, in comparison with a nursery that does not have this appearance.

Parents are rightly wary of 'cut price' childcare, because the fees must also imply that Children Act standards are being cut, and therefore that the nursery is operating outside the legal requirements set down.

For me, the most important issue around fees is that they should not be blamed by nursery staff for lapses in performance. Given that fees for childcare are high – for every parent – it is very simple to say that bookings are not being made because prices are too high. Some parents will not be able to afford the fees and are unlikely to visit if this is their position. However, if after being appraised of the fees the parents visit the nursery, they are then confirming that the service in some way justifies the fees.

A second important issue is not to be over-anxious to correct an imbalance in budgets through increasing fees. As has already been noted, childcare costs are extremely high in any event, and all parents find them hard to afford. Increasing them even further is inevitably to run the risk of losing some children. Compare the effects of:

- a 5 per cent increase in fees;
- a 5 per cent cut in overheads;
- a 5 per cent increase in booked places.

Increasing fees may not always be the appropriate response, and in my experience the other two are *always* worth attempting first. More subtle ways of using pricing would be to vary fees for different services or slots in the week, and to offer prepayment or 'off season' discounts during the summer holiday.

Finally, here is a setting-fees checklist:

- Set fee objectives.
- Don't set fees arbitrarily or by 'feel'.
- Relate fees to your marketing objectives, e.g. when you want to break even, how competitive you want to be, the image you wish to portray.
- Understand market conditions.
- Understand sensitivity to fees by parents.
- Outwit your competitors.

RISK ASSESSMENT

Having worked through this chapter, you will understand that there is little tolerance in the nursery business, regardless of the sector that you are part of. Unexpected staff absences or turnover, supplier price rises, one or two fewer children in nursery, a reduction in children's hours, a new cooker, can all tip the balance of both your books and your ability to develop the service. Being prepared for such risks, and understanding how you can reduce them as well as redress the imbalance they cause, is an important aspect of remaining sustainable. There is also another set of risks to the business, which may be harder to quantify. These are issues such as: new regulations from OFSTED that require a change in the service or additional costs; a crash in the computer system; the fall-out from a complaint about the service brought by a vociferous parent, which impacts on the nursery's reputation locally.

As a nursery manager, you are accustomed to preparing risk assessments of, classically, an outing that you want to undertake with nursery children. The whole operation needs one too.

A risk management schedule should be drawn up to mirror the objectives of the business, and an assessment should be made against this schedule on a regular basis. This will help you to anticipate what risks you may be facing in the coming period, and to plan for them. The first step in this process will be to make sure you are up to date with current issues relating to the management of nurseries. At the end of the book we list useful organisations and websites that will help you to anticipate changes coming down the line.

The goalposts have changed for managing nurseries well; the task no longer concerns making sure only that children's entitlements are met and parents' expectations are assured, although these both remain essential and central. To maintain the long-term health of your nursery today, your plans and actions must demonstrate that:

- The quality of the service provided is both visible and valued by those who use it, particularly where it diverges from the tight, recognised regulatory framework.
- You are working in partnership with others involved in family wellbeing, and are rooted in the community you serve.
- You are an employer of choice for staff, and can therefore provide continuity for children and families.

Chapter 7

Reviewing the service

- Responding to parents
- Managing change
- Quality management
- Employing consultants
- Using advisers
- Outsourcing

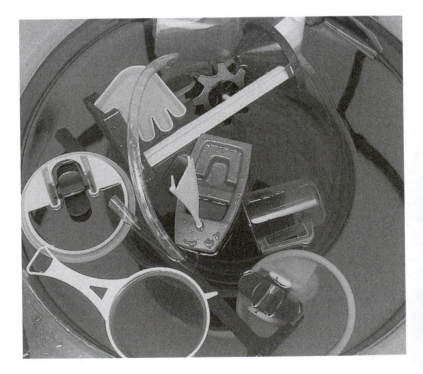

Change in education is easy to propose, hard to implement, and extra-ordinarily difficult to sustain.

Andy Hargreaves, Boston College

It is vital to get the basics in place, but it is also important to understand that excessive emphasis on the basics and standardisation can deny creative and critical learning: these are essential to moving forward, to bringing about real improvement for all children that matters, spreads and lasts.

RESPONDING TO PARENTS

According to the Confederation of British Industry, those who pay for pre-school care and education spend an average of 25 per cent of earnings on the services they procure. If this is what parents are committing themselves to, they want and will see that their hard-earned money is well spent. What do parents expect and wish to see?

All local authorities now provide web-based and/or printed guides to choosing childcare, which all parents can access. The guides typically suggest parents look carefully at:

- training and experience of staff: are they ready to respond to your child?
- safe and clean premises: is there plenty of space to play and explore?
- planned activities: is there a range of toys and equipment each day?
- welcome: were you and your child welcomed warmly from the start?

The guides often provide the most frequently asked questions by parents, typically:

- How long have you (the manager) been working with children?
- How have you learned your job?
- What is it about working with children that you enjoy?
- Can I see all the play space, including outdoors?
- How will you make sure my child has a chance to play outside?
- Where and when will my child rest?
- What kind of food and drink will you give?
- What will my child do all day?

- How do you encourage good behaviour?
- Will my child be with a regular group of children? What is the age range? What if my child's timetable doesn't work in the same way as the rest of the group?
- How will I know that my child is making progress?

The guide is also likely to provide pointers to quality for the parents to check out, typically:

- Are the children calm, safe, happy?
- Do children play and talk together?
- Are the staff listening to children and answering them carefully?
- Are the staff friendly and do they appear proud of their work and of the nursery?
- Are the staff joining in with the children's activities?
- Are there lots of planned activities with a learning focus?
- Can children plan and choose some activities themselves?
- Are there plenty of clean toys and equipment?
- Are the premises clean, well kept and safe?
- Where are the parks/libraries/shops that the children visit?
- Do parents have plenty of chances to say what they want for their children?

The lists above constitute the preparation that all parents can be expected to have, and therefore can also be taken as the basic list of issues for continuous review, to ensure positive responses can always be given.

A different approach to reviewing the service starts with a more aspirational view of what is being provided:

- To what extent does the nursery raise expectations of what children can achieve?
- To what extent can the nursery demonstrate that it continues to improve outcomes for children?
- How agile is the service in its response to the changing community in which it is located?
- What local collaborations has the nursery put in place?
- What is the succession planning process for senior staff?

These are the kind of standards that are permeating the newer, higher qualifications for setting leaders, discussed in Chapter 3.

Finally, your own objectives provide you with a means of evaluating everything you do. The nursery business I set up in the 1990s came up with the following, as a basis for reviewing our service:

- Constant adult/child interaction and conversation, and the impact of a key-person system for children, are continuous requirements throughout nursery life.
- The benefits of what we offer are to provide the children with the ability to participate with others in constructive play, and to be confident in their choices and activities.
- If we are to present ourselves as offering a real option at pre-school age (i.e. ages 3–5), we must be able to demonstrate the principles that underpin our educational approach as well as our managerial ability to put these principles into practice effectively and efficiently.
- We must be able to offer the assurance to parents that our curriculum is built around their priorities and that there is evidence of these being addressed on a continuous basis. We must be able to measure the effectiveness of attending to the identified priorities in terms of the children's development, and in a language that parents can share.

MANAGING CHANGE

Change has become recognised as a necessary component of modern management. It has even become fashionable and in danger of becoming an end in itself.

Development is change and learning in balance. It is a fundamental law of ecology that, for any living thing to survive, its rate of learning must be equal to or greater than the rate of change in its environment. The external environment in which nurseries operate is changing rapidly – politically, socially, economically and academically. We should not increase the turbulence this will cause by over-emphasising the change side of the equation, at the expense of *learning.*

Change, is, after all, part and parcel of a nursery service. If we accept that our service must be parent-based, flexible to individual children's needs, creative and responsive, people-oriented, effective and efficient, it follows that every day is different, every moment incorporates changes.

So why do we need to address or cope with change as a discrete area of concern? This is because, sometimes:

175

- things do not turn out as expected;
- a policy or practice is not working properly;
- a new directive is imposed;
- a new development is discovered;
- change is worthwhile for change's sake.

In other words, changes occur for different reasons. Sometimes change is thrust upon us and at other times we introduce it ourselves. Some of the reasons may be negative. For example, changes made to budgets may be in order to redress a disappointing trend in the accounts; modifications in the activity programme may reflect the impossibility of having sufficient staff to cover all areas of the nursery at one time. There may be a new requirement or recommendation made by OFSTED following an inspection, that does not chime with the nursery's philosophy.

On the positive side, new research into the way children develop may bring about a review of your curriculum, your child observation practice, or the qualities you look for in new staff. A new shift-pattern formula may result in more time for staff discussion with parents. A new member of staff with expertise in a specialist area, say equal opportunities, may introduce radical new approaches to positive image development.

What is our response to change? Usually it puts us into a state of shock, to one extent or another ('Why is this change necessary at all?'). Secondly, we are likely to make a defensive retreat ('Was this really necessary? What is wrong with the way we have been doing it up until now?'). Gradually we begin to acknowledge that the change is probably appropriate, and finally we adapt to it. This process can be handled in order to achieve a change quickly, or slowly, and it can be managed well, or badly.

Generally, people are willing to accept change if they have confidence in themselves in their role, and in their immediate seniors and colleagues, and in the management.

As a manager, you will have a management style, a way of approaching and handling people and tasks, to achieve your objectives. The way changes are introduced into your setting will largely reflect your management style, and you will be judged as being effective or ineffective by others in terms of the introduction of change, in relation to your style. Figure 7.1 provides a scale on which you can assess the way you are inclined towards a particular approach.

Basic style	Effective	Ineffective
HIGH TASK	Seen as knowing what he/she wants and imposing her/his methods for accomplishing this without creating resentment	Seen as having no confidence in others; unpleasant, and interested only in short-run output
HIGH TASK AND RELATIONSHIP	Seen as good motivator who sets high standards; treats everyone differently (as equals) and prefers team management	Seen as a person who tries to please everyone and so vacillates back and forth to avoid pressures from either side
HIGH RELATIONSHIP	Seen as having implicit trust in people; primarily concerned with developing the talents of her/his staff	Seen as primarily interested in harmony and being a 'good person'; unwilling to risk disruption of a relationship to accomplish a task
LOW TASK AND LOW RELATIONSHIP	Seen as appropriately permitting her/his subordinates to decide how the work should be done; and playing only a minor part in their social interaction	Seen as uninvolved and passive, as a 'paper shuffler', who cares little about the task at hand or the people involved

FIGURE 7.1 Basic leader behaviour styles

The nature of change

Being action-oriented, managers of early years' services want to know 'how can I do this now?'. We have noted earlier the disastrous effects that introducing change too quickly can bring. Change is a process of nurturing and bringing out, rather than one of rushing on and hammering in.

Pedler *et al.* (1989)* defined the 'learning organisation' (or the organisation best equipped to cope with change) as 'an organisation which *facilitates* the learning of all its members and *continuously* transforms itself'. There are links with training here, but there are dangers:

> Training is a liability in situations where you have to flex quickly – what price the training you had yesterday because today I want you to do something different? But you will not do it because you are so wedded to what we trained you to do yesterday!
>
> Nick Georgiades, British Airways

Change involves having a respect for all new ideas and valuing what each individual can bring, if given the opening:

> The first thought is that it is [change] about a company, as a priority objective, developing all its human resources, enhancing all their skills . . . but not being content with that . . . learning from those people how the company can be improved . . . so that it becomes a cycle of learning.
>
> Paul Marsh, Jaguar

The rate of external change on early years' services is increasing rapidly. With competition and deregulation being encouraged by the government, childcare providers are continually having to transform themselves to offer higher quality, more affordable and relevant services. Not all of them will make it. Those that do will have realised that the people with the ability to learn what their parents want, and who can respond rapidly to deliver it, will be those who contribute to add value and profitability to the services of the organisation, and ultimately, through the parents' increased perception of the quality of the services, their share of the market.

If people are unready or unprepared for change they will consider it as a problem, and their response will swing between absolute rejection and poor performance in what they are doing. The appropriateness and sensitivity with which change is introduced is frequently of larger concern than the change itself. A well-developed process is the nine-point plan.

1 Getting an authentic picture of the present

This requires us to distance ourselves from the present (problem) to which we have contributed in part, in order that we can openly face the necessary change. We need to create a risk-free environment in which to discuss the issue; that is, not one of criticism or reproach, but 'We are where we are, and where do we go from here?', as an ex-chairman of my own nursery business liked to put it.

2 Developing a common vision

If the majority will commit to a common vision of the future in which they have had a hand, then there is a good chance of creating sufficient organisational energy to achieve it.

The purpose of the change needs to be shared, and it needs to be seen as contributing to, not compromising, the overall objective. Until all staff can share in the overall objective, they may well feel that their particular role is compromised by the change they are being asked to absorb ('We can no longer do what we set out to do in the intended way'). However, what they may not have understood is that, when the change was accepted, they would not have been able to do it at all!

3 Building a bridge between the present and the future

The best way to introduce a change is to draw on a coalition of:

- who *knows* about the problem (the cause);
- who *cares* about the problem (the effect);
- who *can do* anything about the problem (the solution).

4 Launching a 'pilot'

Another way of introducing a change is to test the change within a small group or over a short period of time. This will provide an opportunity for staff to shape the change themselves from the very practical standpoint of 'Does this work better than it did before?'. It will also provide an opportunity to get it right from the outset, rather than risk the upheaval of change, only to find that a further modification is required to see it successfully in place.

5 Communicating the change

There is rarely any benefit in keeping things secret, but there are often disbenefits. For instance, others are denied the opportunity to introduce a good idea, they are precluded from the energy generated from something that works well, they are not given the chance to enthuse.

If the process is shared, then so too is the rigour with which the change is being considered. It has not come about on a whim, or even a prayer, but a well thought-out developed improvement.

6 Encouraging others to join

People have different reasons for involving themselves in the process of change. Some will want to ensure that the balance of micro-politics is not jolted, that territory is not given up to others. Most want to contribute to the greater good of the nursery and enjoy being involved in finding the right solution.

One Japanese company reports that it implements over 5,000 staff suggestions per day. How many has your organisation implemented this year?

7 Reinforcing corporate culture

Charles Handy (1987)* would say that the culture in your organisation is likely to be broadly based on one of the following:

- *one-manager rule,* where information is kept centrally, and the centre cannot easily be challenged;
- *the role culture,* where everyone knows their place and all responsibilities are standardised and accepted, and is slow to change;
- *the task culture,* where people take on specific projects, with deadlines and agreed objectives, releasing a lot of energy from a few individuals;
- *the people culture,* where the focus is on each person being treated equally, but no one individual being able to take a lead.

It is unlikely that your nursery is purely one or another. However, the way change is received will largely be determined by which culture is dominant.

Some key questions to staff could help you identify the broader perception of the nursery:

- What objectives would they use to describe the organisation?
- How would they describe what they would like it to be in the future?
- What happens when things go wrong?
- Who gets rewards and why?
- What releases most energy within the team?

8 Rewarding achievers and others

Commitment from staff is discussed in more detail in Chapter 4, and the relative perceived reward method. Everyone seeks recognition to show that they are a valued part of the organisation. It is the manager's role to ensure that this is positive recognition and in line with the organisation's objectives. 'What can I do to make your work more effective?' can illicit important information for the manager in terms of supporting staff in their response to change.

9 Feedback on the manager's behaviour

Staff are likely to respond best to a manager whose words and action are synchronised. This sounds easy, but many managers expect people to do what they are told, often with little reference to other decisions. It is then not surprising that responses are sometimes contradictory. The incidence of large pay rises and bonuses for directors in the early 2000s, alongside redundancies and outsourcing work to other countries, is a case in point.

Conditions for change

We have already looked at what might constitute an external or an internal change. But there is another type of discussion that affects both the way changes may be introduced and the response such changes will attract.

It is a time of radical policy change, with everything that has come with the Government's *Ten Year Strategy for Childcare**, and although providers have been engaged in this process to an extent, and have influenced the outcome of parts of the policy, understanding how to respond within the context of their own organisations is critical. They must *learn* how to adapt what they do to the needs of the current environment. In Bob Garratt's (1990)* terms, this is part of the policy cycle of organisational learning. Here the manager is rising above day-to-day routines, giving thoughtful leadership and direction as current information is sifted, and in the face of *coups* such as the recent government intervention.

At the operations level, people tend to be so busy and 'heads down' in the nursery that their responses to problems tend to be to do more of or less of what is already happening. This is particularly true when targets or budgets are tightened and priorities have to be readjusted. Performance is monitored against plans and appropriate action is taken through the control systems (see Figure 7.2 and Chapter 6). Ideally, the whole is run like a well-oiled machine – were it not for the deviations from plans that break into the rhythm with unfailing regularity! It is managing these deviations back on to plans that provides the manager with his or her most essential task.

181

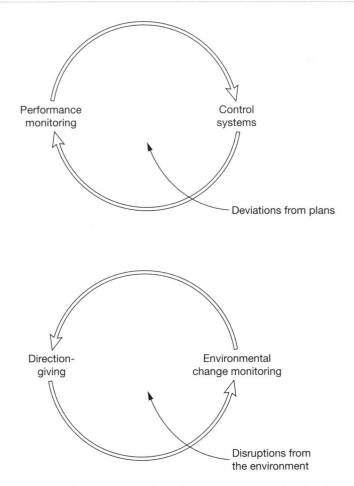

FIGURE 7.2 Organisational learning: the operational and policy
cycles

Effects of change

One of the direct consequences of belonging to an industry providing a
service in which there are so many stakeholders is that the effect of any
change must also be measured in terms of each of their interests. Most
directly affected will be children, parents and staff. However, commercial
life requires that shareholders, employers and developers may also have
their situation changed by what is being introduced.

The reason for the change may be compelling for some stakeholders, but may be unmeasurable for others. This strengthens the case for consultation on the change.

Stakeholders are in the best position to alter the effect on themselves of a change. However, you must be certain about what you are consulting on, in order that their involvement has credibility. Have you decided already, or are you *consulting* on:

- the notion of the change?
- the options for change?
- the mechanics of the preferred option?

Any one of these may be appropriate, but there are few more frustrating situations to be in than being asked your opinion, only to find that the decision has already been taken and that your approval is all that is being sought.

In some instances it may be inappropriate to consult at all. This may be where one stakeholder will inevitably have to stomach a difficult change, for the sake of other stakeholders. It may also arise where individuals find it compromising to be party to a change, and would prefer to abstain (silently).

QUALITY MANAGEMENT

Quality management is sound practice

It is not the intention to prescribe a single quality management system for every nursery's practice. That would defeat the objective of motivating nurseries to think about their own activities and objectives. It is for the individual nursery to develop operating methods in which they have confidence and the ability to satisfy parents about their capabilities. Here we address management matters in terms of good business practice. A nursery's ability to provide assurance about the quality of its services can stem only from systematic control over the particular processes in which it is involved. Such a system would recommend that nurseries periodically carry out internal audits of all matters affecting the quality of the service provided. It is not for the audit to question the professional judgement made, but rather to determine that questions were raised and decisions made and communicated at the appropriate time. The key to a successful management system for any nursery lies in the ability to see that the basis of the process is self-evident through audit, review, feedback and continuous improvement.

Quality management does not need complicated procedures, only sufficient documentation to ensure that roles, responsibilities and relationships are clearly identified and any ambiguity in requirements within the nursery are removed.

Preparation of a quality management system is not something to be rushed. Allow a minimum of 18 months in which to define what the nursery's principal preoccupations are, examine how satisfactorily they are carried out and identify where they could be improved to provide greater confidence in achieving objectives. Draft an improved system, review it with all key staff of the nursery, develop the system and allow time for further review before trying it out under controlled conditions. Set realistic objectives and verify whether they are achieved. When the nursery's principals are satisfied, then gradually introduce the quality management system throughout the nursery, keeping it under review. The important outcome of this process is a positive attitude towards continuous self-assessment, but you can seek accreditation for having a quality management system from the British Standards Institution (BSI).

Costs will be incurred by the nursery at two levels:

- first, in preparing an office quality system manual;
- second, if the object is to proceed to independent certification in assessment, certification and subsequent monitoring fees.

The outlay in establishing and maintaining a high-quality management system should be recovered by the nursery through increased efficiency and competitiveness.

Maintaining the system

The quality management system is a dynamic tool to help your nursery operate with confidence. An essential facet of successful business is to keep the systems used under review and appropriate to the nursery's needs. Nurseries that have gone the route of external endorsement have usually found that the BSI's ISO9000 (British Standards Institution/ International Organisation for Standardisation) quality management system is most appropriate to the service offered.

Documenting the process is vital, so that compliance to requirements is apparent. It entails good communication, ability to trace decisions taken, and responsibility identification at all stages from the day a child starts at the nursery.

The nursery, by having well-qualified and committed people who enjoy their work and having its own management routines in place, will in effect have started to develop its quality management system. The next step is to understand its process better, how people are able or not able to carry out their work, and to start to formalise the nursery's 'informal' method of working.

Start to get help in understanding what quality management means for your nursery by listening to those who have studied the subject and its application in practice – in the care sector. This means investing in education and training.

The nursery will then be further helped by selecting a small group of people – or even one person, depending on the size of the nursery – who will be trained in helping to develop the quality management system. This person in your nursery will be a 'missionary' to everyone else – so make sure that a good communicator is chosen.

The nursery's manager must bring every member – from the most senior to the most junior – into the evolving process and not rely on a few to understand and implement the system. Not successfully promoting the system throughout the organisation is the commonest cause of failure.

The nursery will then formalise its process, with the minimum of bureaucracy, and consequently have better control over that process so that it can improve it continuously. Quality management and certification for quality assurance will come naturally as a result.

A certificated nursery or group of nurseries is licensed to display the National Certification Mark, incorporating the crown, on its business stationery. This provides a public demonstration that its quality management system has been certified by a competent impartial and accredited body. In time the familiarity of the accreditation system will become a valuable marketing aid and achieve international recognition and respect.

Increasingly, when commissioned by others to provide nursery services, for example on behalf of employers, and by local authorities commissioning Children's Centre services, it is increasingly likely that a recognised quality management system will be a condition of contract.

EMPLOYING CONSULTANTS

Consultants are used by organisations and individuals for several reasons. At first sight it may seem strange for a company to employ an outsider to tackle a task that could be done by internal people, and to pay them well to do it, but consider the following reasons:

- Some organisations may not have the necessary expertise among their existing staff to solve a specific problem.
- The expertise may be there but the appropriate people may not be able to fit the assignment into their timetables.
- Even if the right people could take on the task, they themselves might recognise that sometimes an outsider can see problems in a new light and bring a fresh perspective to them.
- Company politics may be such that a disinterested outsider's opinion might more acceptable than that of a staff member.
- A third party, such as an organisation's bank, may insist on an impartial view on a particular issue.
- An outsider can be blamed if things go wrong, and thus keep intact the social bonds existing in the organisation.

Approaches to consulting

In an article 'From expertise to contingency: changes in the nature of consulting', Bob Garratt (1981)* identified three styles in consulting practice: expertise consulting, process consulting, and contingency consulting. Each of these is distinct and, if appropriate for the circumstances, equally valid. It is important to know in which area the consultant is operating as the skills needed for each are different.

Expertise consulting

One use of the 'expertise consulting' approach is when an acknowledged expert in a specific area is asked into an organisation to provide a solution to an already identified problem; for example, the need to design and install an information technology system or a new accounting system. In such a case the consultant's main contact is with the person who asked him or her in to look at the problem – you.

This approach may also take the form of a training course where the expert will pass on knowledge or skills to a staff group, either in-house or on a public programme. Once the course is completed, the consultant will not usually have any further contact with the participants. A good trainer can pass on valuable knowledge and skills, but clearly it is what happens afterwards, within the staff team, that matters most.

186

In his later work, Bob Garratt has likened this approach to surgery; that is, an operation that gives an immediate result, but which cannot always be guaranteed to provide a permanent solution to the problem. It is a drastic, often irreversible, step, because new knowledge is acquired by some individuals, who will undoubtedly want to develop, and others may not be so ready.

Process consulting

Process consulting provides a balance to the logical, rational and often arms-length style of expertise consulting. It involves people much more in their social processes – that is, the feelings and behaviours concerned with a range of managerial problem-solving processes. They often experience a release of energy previously unknown to them.

Working with the emotions in this way may also go beyond the brief envisaged by the manager, and leave the participants fired up with ideas, and with confidence and enthusiasm that the organisation cannot control or accommodate back at the workplace. The relationship between the consultant and the problem-owners becomes quite close during the time they are working together. This can sometimes work against the interests of the organisation as a whole if the participants become alienated from the consultant.

Rather than surgery, this style of consulting may be compared to therapy. As such, it usually needs a complementary approach to enable the participants to develop their newly discovered potential in coping with the 'real' world of their nursery and the problems they face.

Contingency consulting

The aim of the contingency consultant is to become redundant as quickly as possible. This contradicts the conviction held by some that consultants are in business to maximise their fees. The contingency consultant endeavours to make optimal use of the resources already held in an organisation in the form of its staff and their experience. As Bob Garratt writes:

> It attempts to integrate the expertise and process practices when appropriate to the progression of the organisation's problem . . . relying on the asking of high-quality questions and developing an information based approach to problem solving.

187

The contingency consultant, whether internal or external, is neither surgeon nor therapist and is used rarely, like small doses of homoeopathic medicine given only when needed.

It may seem strange that, in using a consultant to help solve a problem, the manager is not buying the expert knowledge of the subject to unravel the problem, but rather his or her intelligence and naivety. In many situations, the issues that look like technical puzzles (yet which cannot be solved by staff) are symptoms of a managerial problem. In this case, therefore, finding the solution often depends on the ability to reframe the question in such a way that the nursery's values are made explicit.

Whichever consulting approach is used – expertise, process or contingency – the test of its quality is whether the manager feels at the end of the exercise that the relationship has been one of colleagues acting in a participative way to resolve organisational issues.

USING ADVISERS

Managing a nursery is a complex and multidisciplinary task. There will be many areas of concern that you can deal with to an extent, and at which you will become accomplished through experience. However, it is critical to be able to identify the point at which specialist help is both prudent and expedient, and to recognise that this will need to be sought externally. This is the start of your business network, your means of maintaining professional contacts and support.

Advisers are so important to the smooth running of a business, however small, that it is vital to employ the right ones. This means not only those who are qualified and experienced enough to do a competent job for you but also those you like and feel comfortable working with.

The bank manager

'Train your bank manager' was one of the first pieces of advice I was given as an owner of a small business. Even though you may not own the nursery, and accounts may not be your responsibility, you are the public face of the business, and the bank will have greater confidence in the nursery if there are open lines of communication with you.

It certainly is worth making an effort to spend time deciding where to base your account and in getting to know your manager. While the bank nearest to you is the most convenient, it may not be suitable for all your needs. For example, a local branch with little experience of small businesses might not provide all the services you would expect, although a far-sighted manager in such a branch may well be very willing to accommodate you and add a little variety to his or her life. A very large branch in a busy city centre may not be prepared to devote what you consider to be the appropriate attention to your comparatively small interests unless it offers specialist advice and services to small businesses.

Therefore, weigh up the advantages and disadvantages of size, personal attention, specialist services and ease of access when choosing a bank. Talk to the bank manager before you place your business account, even if you have banked there personally for years, and discuss the special needs of a nursery. Find out what sort of information the manager will need from you to keep him or her happy; for example, regular cash-flow forecasts as reassurance that, although there may not be much money in your account at the moment, it will be coming in. If you are going to be away for an unusually long time, or if you are expecting a particularly large bill, let the manager know. Do not let the bank be faced with any unpleasant surprises, because bank managers like to know what is going on, and will probably send you costly letters if they do not.

The role of banks has changed dramatically over the past few years. They now offer a wide range of services, many of which are specifically designed for small businesses. So ask questions, and make sure that you know exactly what the bank can do for you. Handle the bank manager as you would a parent – listen to what he or she needs from you, provide it with alacrity, and the manager in turn should look after you. Bank managers can also be a useful source of new parents – provided, of course, that they have a high regard to you and your nursery.

The accountant

Make sure that you work with a properly qualified accountant who will be able to give you advice on tax-related affairs and on preparing a business plan. The accountant should be consulted about how to prepare and submit profit-and-loss accounts, balance sheets, and cash-flow forecasts. This information may also be available from your bank manager.

Bookkeeping services may be provided by an accountant or you may go to an independent bookkeeper. Some nursery managers keep their own books and submit them to the accountant at the end of the financial year for their professional attention and completion. This takes more self-discipline as you really should do the accounts every day rather than wait to complete the books at the end of the year.

A lawyer

Whoever looks after your legal affairs must be a specialist in small business, who will understand the particular issues affecting nurseries. You will not need to use a lawyer's services in setting up as a sole trader, but it would be wise to employ one if you are entering a partnership agreement. If you take the step of becoming a limited company, your legal adviser will obviously play an important part in helping you avoid all the potential pitfalls of commercial law.

Should you become involved in writing contracts for your parents, or if any parents prepare their own, perhaps on behalf of their employer, you will wish to have them drawn up or checked by someone who specialises in contract law. This may be the same person who looks after your other interests. If not, it may be another lawyer within the same practice, or one who is recommended by your usual adviser. There are now legal practices that specialise in standard contracts for payment of, for example, nursery fees. They will also collect debts and take action on your behalf. It is worth using them.

You may also be involved in drawing up or reviewing terms of employment. This area of law is currently moving very quickly, with new European directives almost daily. It is a specialist area, and legal advice should be chosen accordingly.

Again, establishing a good relationship with your legal adviser is important as, on the few (we hope) occasions when you will work together, speed and cooperation may be of the essence.

An insurance broker

You could draw up your own insurance portfolio by reading all the journals in the local library, but it would take a great deal of time. The safest approach is to go to an adviser, and in the UK there are two types to choose from. There are 'appointed agents' and 'independent financial advisers' (IFAs,) and no one person can have a dual role.

Appointed agents represent one insurance company and they can sell the products only of that company. If the company does not have the full range of products, the agent is not allowed to sell you one that is unsuitable.

Independent financial advisers can recommend only the product that is best for you. They must be impartial and must give 'best advice'.

Other sources of insurance advice are the banks and building societies, both of which may be tied to one insurance company. Solicitors and accountants belong to recognised professional bodies. In the UK, the

Financial Services Authority regulates all those who provide financial services.

My experience is that, as with most other purchases, you get what you pay for. The cheapest policy is unlikely to have such broad cover as others. However, you will need advice on calculating the real risks you are facing, and matching a policy to your needs.

There are many 'composite' insurance policies on the market for nurseries and schools, all of which cover the requirements of the Children Act 1989. Optional extras are usually available to cover, for example, non-payment of fees, professional negligence, and staff sickness.

OUTSOURCING

Outsourcing is where an organisation decides to use another organisation to handle work normally performed internally. Small businesses regularly outsource payroll processing and distribution functions, i.e. those processes that are largely transactional, and rely on information supplied and controlled by the business. Outsourcing is usually organised because it is a cheaper way of getting routine jobs done. This may be because the business does not have, or want to take on, the space to do these things, or because it does not want to be distracted by recruiting/training people with specialist skills. There are other quantifiable reasons for outsourcing: you may not want to be distracted from your essential responsibility of managing children, parents and staff to run this function; you may want to get something started very quickly, and not have time to learn how to do it internally. Many businesses now outsource all their HR functions, as this is an area where keeping up with new legislation alone can be all-consuming. Taking this route can ensure that internal HR remains strategic, and personal to those you employ.

This chapter has explored the importance of continuous review, and looked at some of the various ways of going about it. Even if you are not at a point where a quality management system seems appropriate, take notice of the essential, and widely accepted aspects of quality care, and focus on making sure that everything about what you do contributes to improving them:

- well-trained staff who are committed to their work and can tune in to children;
- facilities that are safe, supportive to children, and accessible to parents;

- ratios and group sizes that allow staff to interact appropriately with children;
- provision of instructive learning environments.

Finally, if there is only one question you ask of everything that is done in nursery, let it be 'How does this investment of time contribute to improving the outcomes for children?

The chapter began with a quote from Andy Hargreaves, at Boston College, who has written widely about sustainability in business. We would do well to heed his advice as we endeavour to ensure that our enterprises are built to last:

- Place purpose before profit.
- Preserve long-standing principles in the midst of change.
- Start slowly and advance tenaciously.
- Do not depend on a single leader.
- Grow your own leadership instead of importing stars.
- Learn from experimenting.

As a personal postscript to reviewing the service, I would remind you that today's excellence is only tomorrow's standard and that continuing to provide a quality service requires a connection to the new issues that are occupying the minds of those we serve. The challenge is to build in a process of continuous review that is a cycle of research into practice (see Figure 7.3).

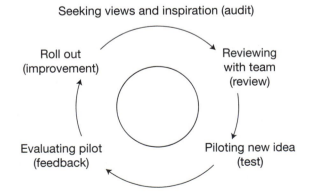

Seeking views and inspiration (audit)

Roll out (improvement)

Reviewing with team (review)

Evaluating pilot (feedback)

Piloting new idea (test)

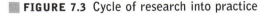 **FIGURE 7.3** Cycle of research into practice

Bibliography and references

Carlisle, H. M. (1979) *Management Essentials: Concepts and Applications*, Chicago: Science Research Associates.

Cohen, B. (1990) *Caring for Children*, London: Family Policy Studies Centre.

Daycare Trust (2006) *RAMPS: A Framework for Listening to Children*, London: DCT www.daycaretrust.org.uk.

Department for Children, Schools and Families (1995–2007) *Every Child Matters*, Crown Copyright.

Department for Education and Skills (2002) *Birth to Three Matters,* November 2002, www.surestart.gov.uk.

Department for Education and Skills (2003) *Research Report RR482*, Queen's Printer.

Department for Education and Skills (2003) *National Standards for Under 8s Daycare and Childminding*, www.surestart.gov.uk.

Department for Education and Skills (2006) *Early Years Foundation Stage*, www. standards.dfes.gov.uk.

Department for Education and Skills (2007) *National Standards for Leadership of Sure Start Children's Centres*, www.surestart.gov.uk.

Garratt, R. (1981) 'From Expertise to Contingency: Changes in the Nature of Consulting', *Management Education and Development*, 12, part II.

Garratt, R. (1990) *Creating a Learning Organisation*, Cambridge: Fitzwilliam Publishing.

Goldschmeid, E. and Jackson, S. (1994) *People Under Three*, London: Routledge.

Handy, C. (1987) *The Making of Managers*, London: HMSO.

Hargreaves, A. and Fink, D. (2006) *Sustainable Leadership*, San Francisco, CA: Jossey-Bass.

Harms, T., Clifford, R. M. and Cryer, D. (1998) *The Early Childhood Environment Rating Scales: Revised (ECERS-R) and Extension (ECERS-E)*, Carrbora, NC: Teachers College Press.

HM Revenue and Customs (2006) *Workplace Nurseries* (2006), www.hmrc.gov.uk.

HM Revenue and Customs *Childcare Vouchers*, www.hmrc.gov.uk.

HM Revenue and Customs *Working Families Tax Credit (WFTC)*, www.hmrc.gov.uk.

HM Treasury (2003) *Every Child Matters*, London: HMSO.

HM Treasury (2004) *Ten Year Strategy for Childcare: Choice for Parents, the Best Start for Children*, www.hm-treasury.gov.uk.

Hodgkinson, C. (1991) 'Education Leadership'. In *The Moral Art*, Albany: State University of New York Press.

Hutton, W. and Davies, W. (n.d) In: 'Trust in Me: The Role of Trust in Leadership', Work Foundation: Campaign for Leadership.

Inner London Education Authority (1980) *Junior School Project*, London: ILEA.

Investors In People (1993) *Investors in People Standard*.

Katz, A. (1994) 'The family is fine . . . but under pressure'. In *Sainsbury's Magazine*, London: New Crane Publishing.

Management Standards Centre, *Management Charter Initiative*.

Munton, T., Barclay, L., Mallardo, M.R. and Barreau, S. (2002) *Research on Ratios, Group Sizes and Staff Qualifications*, London: Thomas Coram Research Unit for Department for Education and Skills.

National Children's Bureau (1991) *Young Children in Group Day Care: Guidelines for Good Practice*, London: NCB.

NCSL (National College for School Leadership), *National Professional Qualification in Integrated Centre Leadership (NPQICL)*.

NICHD (National Institute for Child Health and Human Development) (2002) 'Early Child Care and Children's Development Prior to School Entry: Results from the NICHS Study of Early Child Care', *American Research Journal*, 39, (1): 133–64.

Nursery Education Grant, individual local authority websites.

Pedler, M., Boydell, T. and Burgoyne, J. (1989) 'Towards the Learning Company'. In *Management, Education and Development*, vol. 20, part I.

Penn, H. and Riley, K. (1992) *Managing Services for the Under Fives*, Harlow: Longman.

Reggio Children (1996) *The Hundred Languages of Children*, Reggio Emilia.

Reggio Emilia, *An Educational Project*, http://zerosei.comune.re.it/inter/.

Rodd, G. (1994) *Leadership in Early Childhood*, Buckingham: Open University Press.

Rumbold, A. (1990) *Starting with Quality: Report of the Committee of Inquiry into the Educational Experiences Offered to Three and Four Year Olds*, London: HMSO for the Department of Education and Science.

St Vincent Millay (2001) 'The World is Mine' from 'Journey'. In: *The Selected Poems of Edna St Vincent Millay*, New York: Modern Library.

Stationery Office (2006) *Childcare Act 2006*, www.opsi.gov.uk/acts2006.

Sylva, K., Melhuish, E., Sammons, P., Siraj-Blatchford, I., Elliott, K. and Taggart, B. (2003) *The Effective Provision of Pre-School Education (EPPE) Project: Findings from the Pre-School Period*, London: Institute of Education.

Sylva, K., Stein, A., Leach, P. (ongoing) *Families, Children and Childcare Society (FCCS)*

Whitebook, M., Howes, C. and Phillips, D. (1989) *The National Childcare Staffing Study*, Oakland: USA.

Working Families (2004) *Time, Health and the Family*, London: Working Families.

Working Families (2006) *Is Less More?*, London: Working Families.

Zander, R. and Zander, B. (2000) *The Art of Possibility*, Boston MA: Harvard Business School Press.

Index

4609

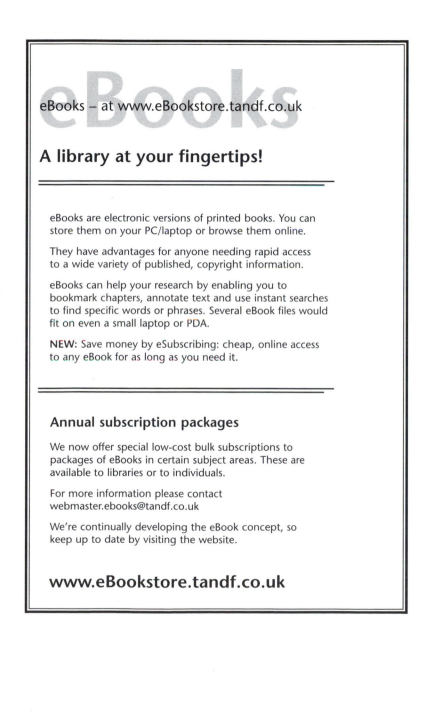